Foreword

The world of initial teacher training (ITT) has been truly frenetic in the past few years and there is no sign that it won't continue to be influenced by the deluge of policymaking that affects the wide learning and skills or post-compulsory sector. We have only to take note of the new funding and governance mechanisms being put into place currently to recognise that all those involved in teaching in this vast system need to keep abreast of such developments and yet maintain the focus of their role in helping people to learn.

This book offers an insight into the world of ITT in the post-compulsory sector. It is a fascinating glimpse into how teacher trainers, many of whom have a long history of involvement in this field, are confronted by the challenges of their daily practice. The contributors write in a personal capacity and their focus, reflections and writing styles shows us how varied this activity is.

The range of topics varies from consideration of learners in ITT and how they cope, including a recognition that some have specific learning needs requiring institutional responses as well as inclusive practice within the sessions themselves, through to institutional issues such as how quality assurance processes could be made more integral to the way in which ITT seeks to develop professional practice. The range also extends to a national perspective on how participation in the Universities Council for the Education of Teachers (UCET) can help inform knowledge of policymaking and its implementation within institutions.

I am struck by how many of the contributors share their concerns about how things are today but instead of simply having a good moan, their reflections are full of opportunity, suggesting ways to engage their learners, or creating ways to experience the feelings that their learners have when confronted with the academic demands of the current series of teaching qualifications. Also captured within these chapters are examples of good practice of tutors involved in teacher training, usually embedded and tacit, even though ironically the focus of their activity is on developing good practice in learning. For example, Paolo Reale abandons his session to discuss the difference that using visual material rather than text based activities has on his trainee teachers, or as we are reminded by Geraldine McCusker that a feminist approach to teacher training has to address those core and deep seated problems of acceptance of the role in society of many women, or of other disenfranchised groups. Sadly, the fact that some of Geraldine's colleagues did not engage in discussion of this important issue shows how challenging the role of critical feminist perspectives continues to be. Karen Lowe's example of a tutor's busy day which is full of research opportunities is a hearty rebuff to those who suggest that research is only for the professionals. Ultimately, we are all professionals and need to reflect and act upon our practice.

I, for one, am going to share this remarkable set of reflections with my colleagues who are also confronted by the challenges and scenarios shared in this book. The voices here can speak to thousands of practitioners who also need not only to look back but to move forward.

Yvonne Hillier, Professor of Education, Brighton University, May 2009

Introduction

This collection represents the reflections of some teacher educators and managers who work in the post-compulsory initial teacher training partnership at the University of Central Lancashire. The partnership has a commitment to reflective practice and as part of this publishes an annual journal of student action research projects called 'Through the Looking Glass'. This journal enables trainee teacher's professional development through writing for publication as well as providing an invaluable resource for new students. As teacher educators we support the professional development of others in activities such writing for 'Through the Looking Glass' and often ignore our own development - we are often so busy 'doing' that we don't make time for ourselves to 'think' and 'feel' connecting with the things that are important to us.

The pieces in this collection have come from a process that supported working collaboratively, enabling us to reflect on our practice both in the past and looking to the future. The physical space was organised as two writing days at the university and as ideas were turned into chapters this was supported by writing feedback. Significantly the reflective space, the ongoing thinking and feeling, has continued from those initial two days creating waves and undercurrents of questions, suggestions and creativity. Almost all of the contributors reflected upon their own skills as writers and this experience prompted some to think how to support the student teachers they taught. As one contributor commented:

> *I've found writing both very difficult and rewarding at the same time. It gives me a true insight into how my students must feel when faced with a lengthy assignment.*

Many described the value of the space to think, something all agreed was lacking in a pressured work environment. One contributor wrote:

> *This was the first chance to stop and think about an issue I have felt strongly about but have not previously written about.*

Others found that they questioned their own practice as they wrote publicly about it:

> *It made me think more about my practice too as I'm making claims about a particular type of practice in a public forum more than in the past so I have to think seriously about the substance of that claim - am I true to it in my own practice?*

We agreed that the end 'product' would hold the pieces but would not impose a writing style or theme. The outcome of this is a variety of voices expressing a range of concerns, thoughts and feelings about teaching and learning. They each provide invaluable insights, in different ways, into the challenges that face us both individually and collectively. This is perhaps not surprising as the partnership has nearly 1800 students being taught at 15 'partner' colleges in the North West of England. It covers a large area, from Carlisle in the north to Stockport in the south, representing diverse student populations. Some of the differences represent the particular local issues which teacher educators have to respond to such as massive unemployment from a major industry which will impact upon a programme. As well as differences there are also huge areas of common concern across the pieces which discuss ways of engaging trainee teachers; of enthusing them and ensuring that they are able to succeed as dual professionals within the diversity of the Lifelong Learning sector. The pieces do not provide answers instead they ask questions to explore an issue taking the reader on this journey. Or, they provide an example of a significant resource, either a reading or a theory, which has inspired or enabled the author to understand and communicate their work more clearly.

The reflective process is about creating change; using our experiences, thoughts and feelings to make teacher education even better. The significance of change is clearly identified by a contributor writing about using research to support professional development for teacher educators:

> *It is time to take stock and identify how I would like to see change implemented and what would be the consequences of such a change. Essentially this is practitioner research in practice - the chance to reflect upon issues and consider strategies to move forward.*

We hope that this collection supports teacher education moving forward and that it will also be used as a resource by teachers and trainees as well as managers in the post-compulsory sector.

Yvon Appleby and Concetta Banks

Authors

Yvon Appleby is a Senior Lecturer at the University of Central Lancashire working in the initial teacher training (ITT) partnership and teaching a variety of post graduate courses.

Concetta Banks is a freelance consultant working with several universities. Until recently she was Programme Manager of Education Studies at Stockport College.

Alison Barton is a Principal Lecturer and ITT Programme Director at the University of Central Lancashire.

Debbie Bentley is a Teacher Educator and Person Centred Counsellor who works at Myerscough College and 'enjoys swimming upstream in the depths of winter'.

Duncan Crossland is HE Curriculum Manager at Stockport College and managed and developed teacher training at the college in the early 90s.

Harold Heath when not working at Wigan and Leigh College splits his time between writing and performing music, collecting guitars, mowing huge garden lawns and working in the local church.

Karen Kay is a Lecturer in Teacher Education at Wigan and Leigh College with over 15 years experience. Her subject specialisms include Biology, Computing and IT, and latterly ITT.

Karen Lowe is HE Manager at Blackburn College, one of the largest higher education providers in FE.

Liz Mayes is ITT Manager at Furness College, which overlooking Morecambe Bay is the furthest west of the partner colleges.

Geraldine McCusker is a Lecturer in Education Studies at Stockport College and has been teaching in this sector since 1992. Her subject area is Psychology and since 2003 has been working in ITT.

Alex Pandolfo teaches at Kendal College and has a background in adult education, work based learning and working with trade unions. He now teaches on the ITT programme.

Paolo Reale has had a varied career at Carlisle College, having been a teacher, Key Skills Co-ordinator, Curriculum Manager and Student Support Services Manager. He is Head of ITT which Paolo describes as the most enjoyable years of his career thus far.

Paul Smith is ITT Programme Manager at Kendal College and has a special interest in access to learning and working with diverse learners.

Contents

'I look up what do I see? Your head on the desk, not looking at me!'

Liz Mayes

As a teacher educator in a small industrial town, life cycle changes, redundancies and ever shifting technologies are our bread and butter. We are able to shape and to change lives, to give new direction to learners and to work with groups whose identity is uncertain. We are also very fortunate in the work that we do; meeting and developing highly skilled, highly motivated individuals who wish to pass on years of experience, to become our teachers of the future. Yet the path they tread and indeed the path we, as teacher educators, tread is not always an easy one as we try to balance the sometimes competing demands of personal confidence and developing new skills to be a teacher.

For some of us, the prospect of change is a challenge to our daily identity. Modern times mean that a proportion of us will change roles and jobs more times than previous generations. Retraining and upskilling are becoming familiar terms and a 'job for life' is now a phrase of the past. Throughout the turmoil, however, there remains a constant, something that will 'rescue' society and facilitate the many changes that we as individuals will encounter: education. It is here that I examine the role of education in managing change both at a personal and professional level. I will examine the difficulties met by Stewart (not his real name) one of our teacher education students as he struggles to cope with a shift in professional identity and the everyday challenges faced by new teachers in further education (FE).

I will focus, in particular, on how many new teaching staff grapple with the professional leap to being involved in examining and reflecting on their own practice, looking particularly at how this manifests itself through the inclusion of action research in undergraduate teacher education programmes. This will include looking at how teacher educators manage this developmental process through our examination of the fictional diary of Stewart, a new trainee teacher who has recently moved into teaching from a small, local engineering company. Rather than talking about disembodied trainee teachers I am using the device of a fictional journal to show the real, and often unspoken, difficulties and challenges that trainees often face. These are often recorded in journals which remain an important but hidden self dialogue about the trials, tribulations and successes of the learning being experienced by trainee teachers. The fictional diary is developed from my experience of teaching students like Stewart and also reflecting on my role in teacher education classes. It is also based on discussions with fellow trainee teacher educators.

Background

For many years previously Stewart was contracted, worked and travelled, spending long periods of time away from home. Stewart has a young family and has recently come into teaching to try and provide a more settled, stable environment for his two young children. Stewart's fictional journal charts his first steps towards becoming a tutor in a vocational subject.

Stewart's Journal

May

Saturday morning, I sit and stare at the letter before me, a presentation? What do they mean by a presentation? They say I can use Power Point or any other suitable supporting resource; what is Power Point…to me it's where I plug the kettle in. I have 10 minutes, I need to be interactive and my title is, 'The Roles and Responsibilities of a Teacher.' A teacher? I don't think I want to be a teacher, perhaps I didn't read the advert properly? Is a tutor a teacher? Surely not, teachers are what we had at school? They were clever, unapproachable and stood at the front, I have never stood at the front…of anything. I don't think I could ever be a teacher. I just want to work at The College, to be nearer to home…

After evenings of sweat and tears, the day has arrived. I sit in front of the guy from HR which I assume is the same thing as Personnel and he seems OK. He tries to smile at me to make me feel better, it isn't working, and then, without warning, I am taken in to meet 'the panel'. After introductions, my 'presentation' begins, I feel naked in the absence of a Power Point but I figure it is best to ignore things I know nothing about than to look foolish. I talk about the job of the teacher as I see it, I base my 'presentation' on the tutors I had at college, what they did, how they supported us; someone has shown me how to look on the Internet and some things have come from there. It's not very good but, in the circumstances, it is the best I feel I can do. I just want it to be over, to leave and forget any notions I may have had about becoming anything other than what I already am.

I decide that I like my job, I can do it, I am comfortable with it. I think about the phone call, about the words they will use when they tell me I haven't got 'the job' but also, I think, what if I do get the job? What will it mean? I watch my mobile all day, waiting for it to ring, hoping it won't, hoping it will? Finally, 4.45 pm…I cannot believe it, they are happy to offer me the position, I start on September 1st. They offer me the opportunity to go in before then, to 'shadow'. I have visions of creeping around in the dark; will anyone know I am there? Little do I know that I will be creeping around in the dark for quite some time to come!

September

It is now the 15th of September, the past 2 weeks have disappeared in a haze of bewilderment and strange terms. My students have been 'screened', I have 'shadowed'; I feel I might survive. I know what I am talking about, I think; the people seem nice and the students, although I am told they are 'learners', seem reasonably happy to be there. Just as things seem to be going OK, without warning, I am called to see my line manager who tells me I am to see the 'Teacher Ed' team. I recall there is a guy in one of the departments called Ed, something to do with 'electrical' perhaps it's him? I consciously think back to my interview, it rings a bell but only faintly. I can't remember what they said; perhaps Electrical Ed and his team are going to show me the Power Point?!

It is a week since my interview with the teacher education team, I find myself struggling to understand how I am a 'teacher' with, as yet unclear, roles and responsibilities and how I am also a student or rather, a learner? I have to attend my teacher education class in the evening, 5 'till 8 and I feel blessed as I believe some classes don't finish until 9! I am fascinated by the rest of the class. At the first session I am curious to know what everyone teaches. We do an ice-breaker and the teacher tells us this is a teaching method; introducing the person next to you and trying to remember as much about them as you can. Some faces are familiar but everyone seems friendly although I am sure that they all know what they are doing and are probably very experienced!

March

The next few months pass quickly, I know about the teaching cycle, my learners' needs are assessed and I can plan to some extent. I know that there are 'right' ways to do things and that 'underpinning' is a term related to the ideas of people that have been there before me rather than something builders do. My methods are limited as are my resources but I feel I am asking questions more effectively as they tell me this is essential in a practical subject. I am not panicking as much although I think I have what is referred to as a disturbed sleep pattern but all around me say that no-one in FE sleeps for the first year. I am aware that I have a dual role, that the term 'dual professionalism' tells me that. Professionalism itself seems to be about how I conduct myself, the language I use and in my previous life I feel I did a professional job. It would appear that doing a professional job and being a professional are very different things. Part of this professionalism, I am told, is being able to reflect on my practice and thankfully, once again, people have been there before me. Cycles seem popular; the teaching cycle and a cycle for reflecting, and the notion of doing things differently next time, although a little confusing and frustrating, is encouraged. Furthermore, writing these frustrations in a journal (apparently not the same as a diary) is suggested as being helpful as these thoughts are often lost as every week seems different.

On a positive note, I can use a text book and the library staff understand me (are probably sick of me) and I can almost produce a bibliography without looking at my handbook, although I still can't remember whether I need to put the page number? I can produce my work on a computer with 3 fingers on one hand but only 2 on the other but I can save and print, I think. The Internet is no longer a mythological 'out there' and I can mark my electronic registers on the same day as the class. In my mind I know the first year is nearly over and 'The summer break' that everyone has been talking about since February is not that far away…

September

The summer is over. I had five weeks off, it took me two to forget work and I spent the final week and a half thinking about going back, at least a week and a half was relaxing! In class it is quite reassuring to see most of the faces from last year, some whom I actually work with, whose similar experiences have kept me going. Our teacher seems pleased to see us which is oddly comforting and thus, year 2 begins…

We are introduced to the first assignment of this second year. Our tutor tells us it is an assignment in which we are required to carry out research. Suddenly the reassuring feeling of the familiar has gone and feels like it will never return. RESEARCH!

The term 'research' conjures up a range of images; test tubes, mad professors or being approached in the local shopping centre by a woman with a clipboard. Surely we cannot be expected to do research? I think back to my old job, the ease and comfort associated with the familiar. The term professionalism and the work we have done on the roles and responsibilities of a teacher leap to mind and somehow, although I am not sure how, a link is made. Do teachers in FE have to do research to 'make' them professionals?

As the lesson unfolds, the panic subsides; we will be thinking about what we do and thinking of ways to improve it. It seems familiar as we were encouraged to work this way in year one, the cycles and diaries, sorry - journals, thinking about how to do things differently. A handout is passed round and I breathe a sigh of relief, I recognise its shape…it's a cycle…I think! Reflect, plan, act, observe; reflect, plan, act, observe etc. We look at it in pairs, it seems to make sense and we discuss what we think it all means. Working in pairs helps as you realise others are still fairly new to the job and have similar experiences and concerns but, as expected, our tutor tells us that working collaboratively (together) is part of developing a professional approach.

We are asked to describe our teaching contexts; where we work, who our learners are and what they are like. We go on to describe a typical lesson and we are asked to say what our partner would see if they were to visit. I remember this approach works well for visual learners and think I must use it more often in my own sessions.

The teacher (a teacher of teachers who teach?) holds up a book, 'Teachers Investigate Their Work', and everyone in the room looks up. We all begin to write frantically; recording the book title and trying to memorise the image on the cover, knowing that, for a split second, we believe that it must hold all the answers! At the end of the session, there will be a mad dash to the library, another 'survival of the fittest moment!'

In the book it suggests how to find your starting point (apparently) so, in our pairs, we are given cards, 4 in all:

- *Is there any question that you have wanted to investigate for a long time already?*
- *Which of your strengths would you like to develop?*
- *Are there any aspects of your work that you find puzzling and which have already been a focus for your reflection?*
- *Are there any situations that cause difficulties and that you would like to cope with more effectively?*

I stare blankly at the questions on the cards, thinking; 'I haven't been here a long time', 'my strengths remain a mystery', 'day-to-day survival is a puzzle' and 'the number of situations that cause me difficulties outnumber the situations that don't!' But as my partner and I begin to talk (apparently known as collaboration) and ask each other questions, things become clearer. There are things we would like to do differently, to change and there are many things we find puzzling. By next week, we have to have an answer!

A week has passed, we are going round the room, each of us telling the group what we would like to improve. We 'focus down' by questioning each other further until our 'issue' can be written clearly in one sentence. I feel elated, I have spent 3 hours in class and have left with one sentence but strangely, I feel a sense of achievement, as though I am on a par with my colleagues even though I am still convinced they are all secretly cleverer than I am!

It is the following week, we are in pairs again. This time we have to consider what we can do in our classroom, or in my case workshop, to address our issues; do we introduce something new, do we change something we do, do we work differently with our learners? Suddenly it strikes me, (apparently there is a name for this, when something suddenly strikes you) - Eureka! My issue is managing large groups in a workshop environment and I have a list of questions that give me good reason to want to address this issue. My idea for addressing my issue is …TO WORK IN PAIRS!!! We have been doing it for weeks! If my learners work in pairs, I will only have to check on 10 pairs and not 20 individuals? Brilliant!

Over the next few weeks we examine different ways of checking, that what we do is working. Apparently it is best to do this in either two or three different ways as this will make our findings stronger. Our tutor describes our research as changing something we do, intervening in the practice of our learners. This intervention is like a platform, to better teaching and like a real platform it is more stable with two legs than one and even more so with three legs than two; the legs are our ways of checking things are working and we have several choices. We can watch what happens, ask the learners what happens and ask ourselves what happens. When asking the learners there are different ways; questionnaires, interviews, reflective statements, journal entries, focus groups and some other more creative ways with drawings and sketches. During my 'collaboration' with my partner, as my work is practical, it seems to make sense to watch what the learners do, to observe. We also figure out that as we are keeping a journal of our own, this could constitute asking ourselves? We decide to go for a third method to strengthen the platform further; we are told to picture a triangle, like scaffolding or a tripod, and with collaboration in mind, I choose a focus group.

We look at recording what we see, what they say, what we say and what we ask. We look at other people's examples from previous years and this helps immensely. Tonight's session is going to be particularly important for me, data analysis; I am keen to attend as I am unsure what my data would look like or what it would tell me. Our tutor gives us a set of drawings, quite a few in fact, and we work in small groups to 'analyse' them. We are told that they are from a group of school children who were drawing their representation of how they see their education, particularly their teachers. We find ourselves engrossed, sitting on the floor, surrounded by drawings. What is fascinating is some of us see completely different things from others: we group our drawings, discuss our reasons, talk amongst ourselves and then regroup them. This goes on for quite some time and it is intriguing to hear what others see! Finally we are finished and we explain to the other groups why we have what we have. Our tutor tells us that here we have identified categories, themes and once again, there is a sense of achievement and a moment where things are clear (reflect, plan, act, observe; reflect, plan, act, observe?). Unbeknown to us at the time, we have presented and analysed data, worked collaboratively, changed our minds and arrived at a consensus even though we all saw things differently!

The next few weeks pass in a flash; all I think about is my research. My time is spent reading, picking out things that might be useful, drawing up observations schedules to record what I am seeing and looking at my classes, thinking about how it all fits together. I have several individual tutorials with my tutor and although these are really helpful, I cannot help but wonder whether she is sick of us all, of me, of constantly reiterating, reassuring and calming…?

....

The difficulties we face as teacher educators are multi-fold. From Stewart's experiences we can see that the transition into education, both personally and professionally can be difficult to manage; moving into the role of 'teacher' and the notion of professionalism is often hard to negotiate. Yet there are many things, as the teachers of teachers that we can do to help our learners navigate this journey on their way to becoming professional educators. Encouraging our learners to become involved in action research can provide a 'situatedness' that demands an examination of current practice, albeit relatively new practice, that can help to develop reflective, professionally orientated skills.

As teacher educators we need to recognise, perhaps even remember, the early days of our own practice and how previous new teachers and indeed ourselves have moved on. How we are now able to think intuitively about what we do and how we have our own theories based on our values and experiences. McIntyre (1980, in Calderhead and Gates, 1995: 44) looks at how reflection can be much more difficult for new teachers than for experienced teachers as their experience is limited:

> *…although reflection has only a limited importance as a means to learning for the student teacher, learning to reflect must surely be an important goal for student-teachers, since it is through reflection on their own teaching that they will increasingly with experience be able to continue learning.*

McIntyre (1980) also considers that it takes time for student teachers to be able to relate their practice to their values around education and that a true critical level of reflection, even through involvement in action research, may never be achieved unless theorising about the practice of others, takes place. By introducing collaboration into the early stages of the action research process, it may be possible to kick start this notion intrinsically; to plant the seed of collegial enquiry at a level that McIntyre considers to be the 'technical' and 'practical' levels. On a similar note Michael Eraut also considers that teachers will:

> *…go on developing their theorising capacities throughout their teaching careers, they will be genuinely self-evaluative and they will continue to search for invent and implement new ideas. Without it they will become prisoners of their early experience, perhaps the competent teachers of today, almost certainly the ossified teachers of tomorrow.*

(Eraut, 1994: 71)

As teacher educators we recognise the enormity and significance of early experiences and the influence these can have on our values and beliefs about what we now do for a living. We also appreciate that the 'ossification' of teachers is not uncommon, years of bureaucracy, changing pressures, the machinery of Government and the seeming reduction of educational standards across the board all take their toll. Amidst all of these issues, how do we keep fresh and inspired; this is a question raised by other chapters in this book.

At an early stage, we need to provide the catalyst for developing our learners' *theorising capacities'* (Eraut, 1994) to equip them for the ever-changing world of FE; we need to furnish them with the skills needed to survive. It is here that we can consider the value of action/practitioner research and the transferable skills learners will develop to help them cope with every day pressures. Barnett (2000) uses the concept of a *'super-complex world'* in conjunction with Wenger's (1998) *'identity formation and learning'* model. This is where modes of belonging, i.e. engagement, imagination and alignment, encourage learners to negotiate through their own experiences the creation of relationships that will help to create their own professional identity. Here, we need to learn as much as we can about our learners' experiences both past and present as these will form the basis of how they perceive the world; the 'super-complex world' around them.

For Stewart, the creation of such relationships i.e. working collaboratively in a 'community of practice' has proved immensely helpful. Sharing thoughts and experiences within the classroom environment has enabled him not only to make links between theory and his practice but also to share his experiences. In addition, there is a collegial aspect whereby all are equal in the 'newness' of being involved in a research culture. A community of practice has developed and the 'super-complex world' of FE is becoming less so as trust is built and relationships formed with both colleagues and tutors. Angela Brew talks of the importance of building a trust relationship with our learners, and they with us in order to *'guide'* them through *'…times of confusion and uncertainty'* (Brew, 2006: 119). It is here that we, as teacher educators, need to take responsibility for supporting learners, our trainee teachers, as they begin to share their fears and anxieties.

We can also encourage our learners to question each other and this verbal sharing of thoughts and ideas can really help the reflective process. Working together can also help learners to verbalise the thoughts initially borne from their reflective/research journals. By encouraging learners to keep a reflective journal, as in Stewart's case, they are able to record thoughts, feelings and fears and 'lay open' concerns about working practices and the newness of the role. Tann (1995, in Calderhead and Gates, 1995) considers that personal theory becomes equated with professional thinking which is at the heart of developing a professional identity as a teacher. Knowles (1989, in Calderhead and Gates, 1995) ponders this further through observing that if journal writings are shared then reflexive practices of writing and dialogue enable the thinking and the contexts in which the constructs are developed to be exposed for scrutiny and discussion. It is a dialogic and reflective process which supports learning, both our own as well as the trainee teachers closing the gap between teaching and learning.

As the teachers of teachers we need to take the time to work *with* our student teachers to learn about their experiences, elicit their educational values and encourage collaborative practice. Through sharing these very personal things as part of the action research process we can help to cultivate the skills that are essential to the development of a professional approach to the role of being a teacher in further education.

References

Altrichter, H. (2008) *Teachers Investigate their Work*. Oxon: Routledge.

Barnett, R. (2000) in A. Brew (2006), *Universities into the 21st Century - Research and Teaching - Beyond the Divide*. Basingstoke: Palgrave MacMillan.

Brew, A. (2006) *Research and Teaching- Beyond the Divide.* Basingstoke: Palgrave Macmillian.

Eraut, M. (1994) in P. Huddleston and L. Unwin (2007), *Teaching and Learning in Further Education Diversity and Change*, (3rd edn). Oxon: Routledge.

Knowles, J. (1989) *Life - History Accounts as Mirrors: A Practical Avenue for the Conceptualization of Reflection in Teacher Education*, in J. Calderhead, and P. Gates (1995) (Eds), *Conceptualizing Reflection in Teacher Development*. London: The Falmer Press.

McIntyre, D. (1980) *Theory, Theorising and Reflection in Initial Teacher Training*, in J. Calderhead and P. Gates (1995) (Eds), *Conceptualizing Reflection in Teacher Development*. London: The Falmer Press.

Tann, S. (1995) *Eliciting Student Teachers' Personal Theories*, in J. Calderhead and P. Gates (1995) (Eds), *Conceptualizing Reflection in Teacher Development*. London: The Falmer Press.

Wenger, E. (1998) in A. Brew (2006), *Universities into the 21st Century - Research and Teaching - Beyond the Divide*. Basingstoke: Palgrave MacMillan.

Learning from the Prestolee School experience

Harold Heath

Introduction

I have been in teacher education for nearly 20 years. My current role as Head of Teacher Education in a large general further education (FE) college, in the North West of England, has evolved with many strands to it. Besides the usual managerial tasks and teaching load, I am regularly asked to work with college staff to improve their practice, or deliver staff development seminars on issues like: 'Inspirational Teaching, What Makes a Good Teacher or What is a Grade 1 Lesson?' This chapter is designed to help and encourage both new and more experienced teachers who sometimes struggle to make sense of what they do due to the many pressures placed on them today from a variety of sources. This chapter draws on the work of Edward O' Neill who faced similar challenges during a different era in teaching. It asks what lessons and inspirations can we gain from such practitioners and their philosophies in today's teaching climate.

Edward O'Neill and Prestolee School

In 1918 a fresh, young teacher took a headship post in a small mill town just outside Bolton and although it is nearly 100 years since Edward O'Neill began his work in Prestolee School, many of the issues he faced then are still with us today in 2009. The success of his life's work makes fascinating reading and offers much in the way of encouragement for modern practitioners. Like teachers today O'Neill was faced with challenging learners, complex social issues, disinterested parents and employers and worst of all an oppressive, outcomes driven regime.

That Prestolee School became a huge, national success was due largely to O'Neill's philosophy on teaching and learning, coupled with his relentless enthusiasm. Those in the teaching profession who are genuinely interested in maintaining a professional 'freshness' would do well to learn from the lessons of an experiment that shook the foundations of the prevailing system of state administered education. What was it that made Prestolee such a success and could understanding this inform teachers of all disciplines and experience today, particularly in terms of professional freshness and pedagogical integrity?

Gerard Holmes in his book about Prestolee and O'Neill entitled 'The Idiot (sic) Teacher' described the school as being:

> *A place where children were able to develop their innate characteristics - trustfulness, helpfulness, discovery, activity, initiative, concentration, gregariousness - and grow into well informed, conscientious resourceful companions.*

(Holmes, 1952: 2)

Even the most cursory examination of these principles should give the reader a sense of excitement and wonder when they are compared with the often flat, technical and sterile mission statements of many of today's educational institutions. O'Neill clearly loved working in a busy and vibrant environment that made the most use of space and resources to create learning opportunities for the children. This phenomenon is well documented by Burke who describes O'Neill's:

> ...*challenge to the notion of physical and pedagogical space of the classroom as being both radical and revolutionary in a system that had changed little since the 'payment by results' era.*

(Burke, 2005: 264)

In fact O'Neill discusses, often and in agonising tones, his own teacher training and early years as a novice practitioner where he was expected to join the ranks of the 'factory' model of teaching as they went through the daily grind of cramming information into the minds of the more or less unwilling but subservient learners. Rather like Mr Gradgrind in Dickens' Hard Times who insisted that:

> *What I want is, facts. Teach these boys and girls nothing but facts. Facts alone are wanted in life. Plant nothing else, and root out everything else. You can only form the minds of reasoning animals upon facts: nothing else will ever be of any service to them. This is the principle on which I bring up my own children, and this is the principle on which I bring up these children. Stick to facts, Sir!*

(Dickens, 1854: 47)

And just in case it may be supposed that such philosophy disappeared with Dickens, only recently a teacher was heard to reply to the question 'what do you do for a living' with the answer, '*I flog dead horses*' (Conversation with local high school teacher, October, 2008). It was against this prevailing philosophy that O' Neill developed a system of education based on practical activity and self discovery maximising every inch of space available in the school. One of the many home made school mottos that O'Neill had emblazoned on the walls of the school read '*It's geese that need stuffing not children*' (Holmes,1952: 184) thus laying bare his view that education should have a liberating and not a nullifying effect on a person's life.

Rogers expresses a similar view when he affirms:

> *I want to talk about learning. But not the lifeless, sterile, futile, quickly forgotten stuff that is crammed into the mind of the poor helpless individual tied into his (sic) seat by ironclad bonds of conformity! I am talking about LEARNING - the insatiable curiosity that drives the adolescent boy to absorb everything he can see or hear or read about gasoline engines in order to improve the efficiency and speed of his cruiser.*

(Rogers, 1983: 18)

Although O'Neill's views pre-dated Rogers by half a century and both men were, geographically speaking, oceans removed from each other, O'Neill, like Rogers, saw the potential of children being stifled by a regime that based its teaching and learning more on military drill than on loving-kindness, and one which he confessed to being an unwilling contributor. In 1918 he addressed a conference at Oxford on 'New Ideals in Education' and told his listeners that:

> *I have taught in a room with four classes of over fifty boys. On my right fifty boys voices announced that: 'rats, they fought the dogs and killed the cats' whilst on my left, fifty other boys bellowed that, 'the little revenge ran on, sheer into the heart of the foe'. I have flogged all round the class. I have been skilled in the Punch and Judy show style of teaching, 'hands up, hands down,' and adept at chalk and talk… I have fought for and had results.*

(O' Neill, 1918: 110)

Clearly, such a view of teaching based on a philosophy that suppressed students and stifled learning moved O'Neill to experiment in creating an approach to education that placed the learner at the centre of the enterprise and valued their individual human spirit as being something unique and worth celebrating. This was at the heart of what kept O'Neill 'fresh' and motivated throughout his long career in teaching. Primarily he loved teaching and never lost sight of the responsibility before him in the shape of those tiny faces, each with their own story, for Prestolee School was built in the shadow of a huge mill which employed children as 'half-timers'. O'Neill said that to him each window in the mill was like a monument of lost opportunity for the children it used and it was his desire to create opportunities for the same children to break free from those chains. O'Neill describes in many instances the challenging issues brought to school by his learners (O'Neill, 1918: 111-116). However, he had many responses to those who wanted to dragoon and press gang him into a world of lethargic and unfulfilling practice.

Of course there will be many voices today who may argue that such a view is unrealistic, naïve and simply unachievable in contemporary educational settings. It will be pointed out that modern teachers are governed closely by managers who are themselves watched relentlessly by government who are paranoid about producing statistics to show that things in the education garden are looking good and getting better. Besides the unfortunate possibility of producing generations of unsatisfied learners, many teachers have left the profession for largely the same reason - a sense of dissatisfaction. In December 2007 the BBC ran an article claiming that, '*more than 250,000 qualified teachers no longer work in England's schools*' (BBC News UK). One wonders whether they faced the same questions that O'Neill faced in the early part of the 20th Century, but were unable to come up with any solutions.

Likewise, teachers should never forget that although they are ready to teach, their students may not be ready to learn. Like O'Neill they are faced with many and varied social issues that are unavoidably brought into the classroom or workshop which can make the job of teaching a challenge and an opportunity. Watchwords like 'retention and achievement' can be heard along every corridor and meeting room in FE institutions, and with funding now well and truly linked to benchmarked performance, an O'Neill style approach to teaching might certainly assist those teachers who need a supply of encouragement and inspiration to help offset the demands of the job.

As Burke (2005) points out it was probably during his training as a teacher at Crewe that O'Neill was introduced to Dewey's (1897) pedagogic philosophy and the notion of education being as much a process as a product. This undoubtedly helped shape his thinking. He resolved that although he was part of a mainly unsatisfactory system of State controlled education; he would make the confines of his own classroom, and later school, a place where learning flourished. And this he determined from the outset was not going to be solely teacher driven. Using what the students had or were interested in became a feature of O'Neill's approach to learning. Basically he reasoned that if you could find out what was relevant in the life of the learner then that is a powerful motivator to learn. O'Neill was brilliant at this and his school became a wonder-world of adventure, excitement, discovery and self-starting initiative. Not only did he not have few problems with truancy but the learners developed a desire to learn.

In fact the students loved school and could not wait to arrive to continue the work from the previous day. No retention problems there. School was a place where a person could derive a lot of learning from a day's work. And herein lay the secret of the success of Prestolee. Instead of students learning Gradgrind-like facts and figures to apply in some random fashion some day in the future, the learning came as a natural by-product of the doing. The children were always actively doing work on some product or another and from that self-initiated work came the necessary learning.

One of the most striking examples of this is recounted by O'Neill himself describing one of his students named Herbert Frankland. Faced with the prospect of another sibling in the family Herbert confessed that bed time was not an experience to look forward to as space in the family home was severely restricted with children having to share beds. O'Neill worked with Herbert's 15 year old brother and records, '*I got the eldest boy to make a single bed for 1s 6d (7.5p). I call that education*' (O'Neill, 1918: 111). Of course O'Neill was something of a maverick who did not totally relish orders from above but yet he managed to fulfil the demands of the 'Inspectors' and keep alive his dream of a place where education became a wonderful and natural thing, a '*school without tears*' (Burke, 2005: 1).

Examples of his work with students are well documented in 'The Idiot (sic) Teacher' (Holmes, 1952) and were ambitious to say the least. He decided to dig up the school playground and create a garden that would provide endless learning opportunities for the children. Children wrote stories and published their own books. They made the books from scratch and assembled the whole thing with great care and attention to detail, complete with illustrations. Each classroom had a piano and singing was greatly encouraged. Books, books and even more books were purchased for the children and parents who together returned to learn in the evenings. Each morning O'Neill would buy newspapers and post them around the school walls for all to read. Students would be allowed time each day to access the breaking news.

Probably his most ambitious project was the Prestolee School version of Blackpool illuminations, a huge undertaking that gave rise to fantastic learning opportunities. And, yes, the children performed the majority of the tasks under supervision of course from the teaching staff. People came from near and far to visit this spectacle and paid good money into the school funds, except village people who were allowed a discounted entry fee. Such were some of O'Neill's ideas to generate a place of powerful learning and which kept him ever fresh and vibrant, right up to his retirement in 1963.

Unfortunately, after he retired and a new Head was appointed, the school reverted back to a more traditional institution. The garden was replaced with a tarmac playground, the adventure playground, windmill and wishing well (all built by children) were dismantled. New desks were purchased to replace the ones that O'Neill had turned into shelves for books and work benches for projects and the all sacrosanct time table was re-hung back on the wall instead of a picture of the Laughing Cavalier (Hislop, 1997) that O'Neill had replaced it with.

Conclusion

In conclusion what lessons can be learned from this incredible experiment from so long ago? I would suggest that three main aspects of the Prestolee experiment can be usefully considered by today's teachers in terms of good practice and as a sure antidote to professional stagnation.

Firstly, the importance of a personal credo for teaching. What are your core values? Why are you in the job and most importantly, where do the students fit in your scheme of things? A student teacher recently described what was to him, an incredibly profound and worrying issue. He said that he had suddenly been arrested by the terrible thought that the curriculum had become more important than his learners. Take some time to write your personal credo, perhaps reference to Dewey's pedagogic creed (Dewey, 1897) might help start the process. Think about proverbs you could create to best describe your approach to teaching and learning.

Here are a few that O'Neill (in Holmes, 1952: 186) had displayed around the school:

- The best way to learn is to live.
- Real poverty is lack of imagination.
- Let teachers be human, they are not parrots, let them come off their perches.
- Let teachers be spacious.

The problem with education today is the 'idiot' teacher for whom no problem exists:

- Who expects children to do what he/she him/herself can't do - learn.
- Who can only do what he/she has done.
- Who only wants to teach his/her subject.
- Whose qualification is that he/she has passed his/her exams.
- Who is repetitive and uncreative.
- Who has never lived.
- Who has a bus to catch!

Secondly, despite the seemingly oppressive system that you have to work and comply with make the space where you teach your own learning zone. It's your space and you can make it as inviting of the curiosity of your learners as you wish to do so.

O'Neill made the most of the space he had available. Try and experiment with learning arrangements that include furniture. Don't accept tradition for the sake of it. Despite the increasing demands of legislation and paperwork, get your learners out of the classroom occasionally and arrange learning experiences for them which really do broaden knowledge.

Thirdly, rather than having your learners *'tied with iron clad bonds of conformity'* as in Rogers (1983: 18-19) description, design activities for them in which they have some input and control. Never underestimate the power of consulting with students. And for those who are sceptical of such an approach, read the experience of Summerhill School, (Neill, 1971) another inspirational read that has sadly been forgotten. Students, who are active, engaged and doing work which is relevant to their lives rarely present behavioural problems and the issues generally associated with poor retention and achievement.

In addition to this, teachers who seek to apply the above aspects of O'Neill's approach to their work potentially gain the benefits of seeing their students perform wonderfully well, becoming strong autonomous learners. It might mean, however, that occasionally you might miss the bus, but without doubt it is this professional integrity that keeps teachers 'fresh'.

References

BBC News.co.uk, http://news.bbc.co.uk Accessed 16.01.09.

Burke, C. (2005) The school without tears: E.F.ONeill of Prestolee. *History of Education*. May 2005 Vol 34 No. 3.

Dewey, J. (1897) 'The school journal' in R. Ardambault (Ed.) *John Dewey an Education*. Chicago: University of Chicago Press.

Dickens, C. (1854) *Hard Times*. London: Penguin Ed.(1969 reprint).

Hislop, I. (1997) *School Rules*. BBC Channel 4.

Holmes, G. (1952) *The Idiot Teacher*. Nottingham: Faber and Faber with Spokesman Publishers.

Neill, A.S. (1971) *Talking of Summerhill*. London: Gollancz.

O'Neill, E.F. (1918) *Report on the conference of new ideals in education* 12-19 August. LIV Papers.

Rogers, C. (1983) *Freedom to learn in the 80's*. Colorado, Ohio: Merrill.

'Glimpsing the whole at a glance': Using pictures and images to help teacher trainees make sense of the action research journey

Paolo Reale

I've been Head of Teacher Education at Carlisle College for almost 6 years now. This is after 12 years as a lecturer in Tourism, Sports and Leisure Studies, Business and Management, Key Skills and then the Manager of Student Support Services - so a varied career to say the least.

I now teach on both full and part-time Certificate/Post Graduate Certificate in Education (Cert Ed/PGCE) programmes and have found these last few years the most rewarding in my working life. I used to think I was a pretty good teacher until I started learning how to teach others to teach. It's a sobering realisation that you weren't as good as you thought you were. As a teacher trainer, it's vital to try to model good practice. This has been the biggest challenge of the last half dozen years, but one that I've relished.

There is no feeling like observing a student of yours, confidently teach a class using skills and techniques you've taught and indeed shown them in your classes. Not only have they benefited from your efforts, so have their students. As a result the extent of your influence as a teacher educator is truly humbling as it must impact, in some way, on the learning experiences of hundreds if not thousands of students. Consequently, getting it right in the classroom, reflecting on what I do by asking myself, am I doing all I can to create the best teachers I can, underpins my professional practice.

In my teaching I've become increasingly conscious of the use I make of pictures and other visual representations to help my learners 'see' ideas, theories and assessments that are nearly always presented using words. Most theories used in the assessment criteria tend to be weighty tomes and for the average student the wording can be impenetrable. Through using pictures and images in teacher training classes I try to show students the value of what I term a 'visual hook'. Usually this hook is a simple pictorial representation of something quite complex or linear in nature which gives many students a much needed *'glimpse of the whole at a glance'* (Black, 2002: 3 cited in Weber and Mitchell, 1996).

While the use of these pictures and images has been largely instinctive and has developed as I've grown as a teacher, I acknowledge that there is a growing recognition of the effectiveness of such an approach to aid learning. There is something vaguely amusing about this, but quoting directly from probably the most cited author on my teacher training programme has a strange symmetry. However there is a reason for his popularity. A lot of what he has to say about teaching and learning is worth considering and he uses a lot of pictures and images to help him say it. Petty (2006) explores pictures and visual representations in some detail in his latest book and contends that they are: '...*one of the most powerful routes to understanding that research has uncovered*' (p 113). He calls a number of visual representations for learning; *'graphic organisers'* and states that these:

'…greatly help most dyslexic and very right-brain learners' (p 113). Moreover, as he goes on to say, and as I often repeat to my trainees; *'…but all students have a right-brain…so all students will find them useful'* (Petty, 2006: 132).

At this particular moment in time I have just finished teaching the first two classes for the Level 2 and 4 Action Research module. My students are on the part-time Cert Ed and PGCE and this is the first module of their second year. The group are largely made up of vocational teachers, a number from Beauty Therapy, Travel and Tourism and Sports Studies and two from a group of ten are graduates; one in Sports Studies and the other in History.

For this chapter I thought it might be useful to explore and reflect upon how I might make use of pictures and images to help these particular learners understand the action research journey. This is a module often seen by students as the 'most academic' module because of its scientific research nature. All but two of the trainee teachers are doing the Level 2 Cert Ed and none of these see themselves as remotely academic. In fact when one of them had a glimpse at this module prior to the classes she said 'Is this the sort of thing university geeks do?' This prompted me to consider how when introducing the idea of action research I could help dispel the idea that all research was something only clever people did and that it was all rather abstract and otherworldly.

Planning for the first couple of classes

My initial idea was to systematically examine my use of pictures and images with this group of learners, to support my on-going delivery of the whole of the action research module. In so doing I was going to 'model' the very process that I hoped to be teaching them. In the event, this chapter isn't going to be about that, instead it is going to be a reflection on the events that occurred in the second lesson of the action research module. The reason for this is what happened in this class illustrates perfectly why we as teachers should make changes to our practice and challenge the status quo by relying on our teacher intuition. In so doing, as I describe, we leave the door open for things to happen that we did not expect and if we're lucky they can have a profoundly educative affect on us and our students. These events force you to truly reflect on what you're doing and ask yourself 'what just happened and how might it affect my future practice?'

In planning for the first lesson 'What is Action Research?' I thought I would begin by developing an image I'd first introduced to these learners a year ago. The image is a visual representation of what the programme 'looks like' and I have used it at the start of each module to show them how each relates to each other and progresses from each other. In this case the image is a spiral with 3 loops, each representing one of the three modules. Together we would annotate the image as each module was introduced. This way the image grows and develops as the course itself does. This image is illustrated below in Figure 1.

Figure 1. What Year 1 of Teacher Training Looks Like

A Spiral Curriculum!

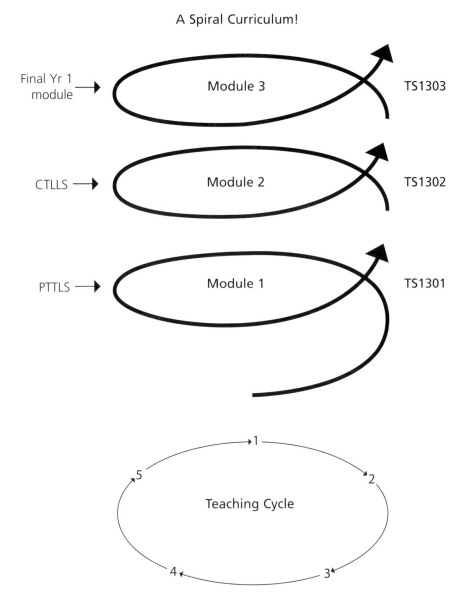

Now embarking on the second year, I needed to show how the year two modules linked to those in the first year. The spiral was no longer appropriate and I also wanted to show that there was a link to the students' further development as newly qualified teachers once the teaching qualification had been finished. This image is illustrated below in Figure 2.

Figure 2: What Teacher Training 'Looks Like'

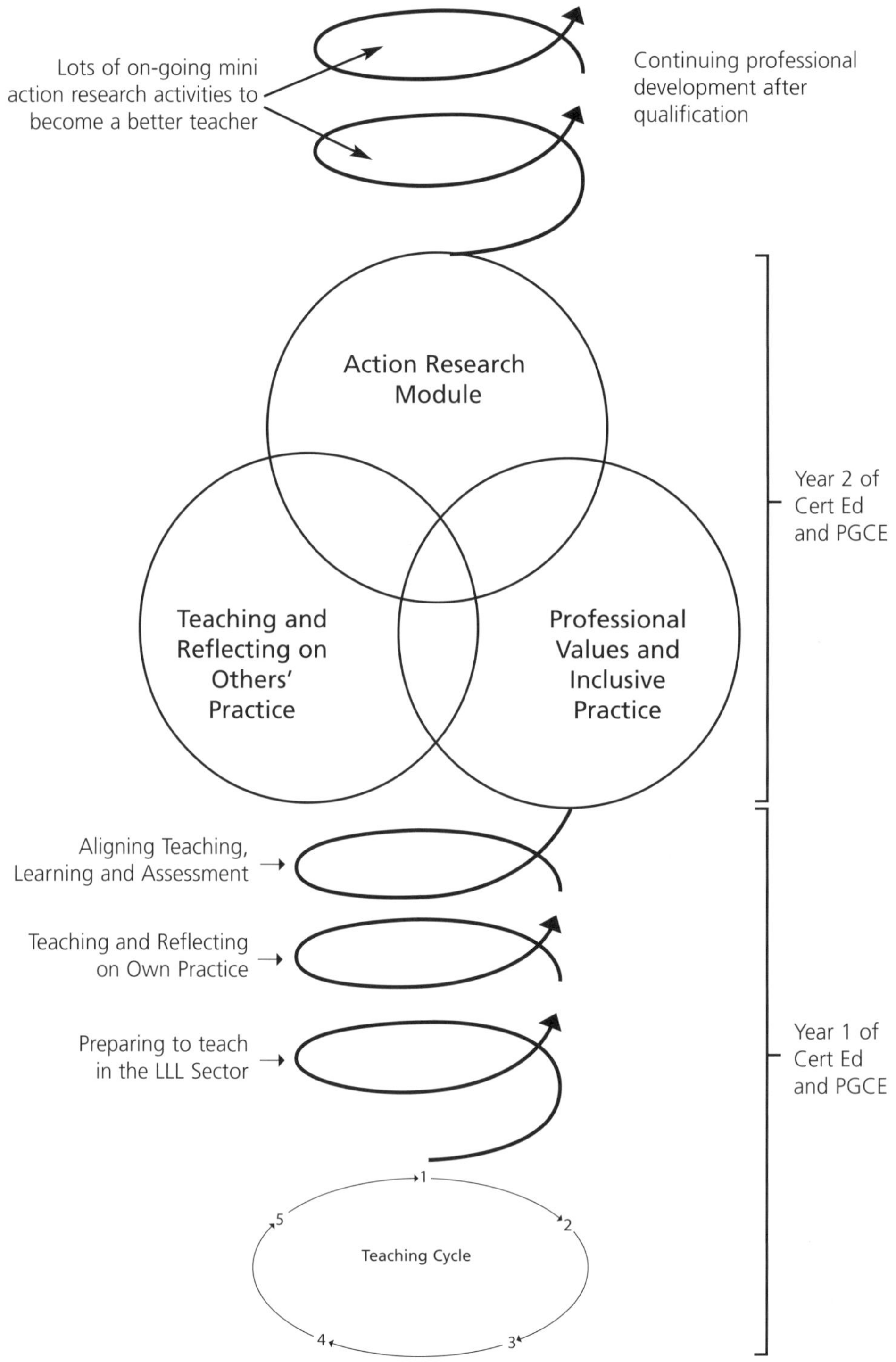

Lots of on-going mini action research activities to become a better teacher

Continuing professional development after qualification

Action Research Module

Teaching and Reflecting on Others' Practice

Professional Values and Inclusive Practice

Year 2 of Cert Ed and PGCE

Aligning Teaching, Learning and Assessment →

Teaching and Reflecting on Own Practice →

Preparing to teach in the LLL Sector →

Year 1 of Cert Ed and PGCE

1
5
2
Teaching Cycle
4
3

This helped in highlighting the 'bigger picture' and gave the trainee teachers a visual representation of what they'd done, where they were going and how things would change in terms of what was to come. What worked particularly well was the 'top bit' of the new image. Here, in showing how the nature of action research continued on beyond their teaching qualification and into their fledgling professions, I was also able to introduce what action research is. To continue to grow and develop as effective teachers, trying new things in the classroom, reflecting on their impact and learning from these experiences was something that should happen throughout their careers. In fact it was happening already to these trainees. As a consequence they could relate to this element of my image and what it represented. They just hadn't known that it was called action research. Now, with the help of my image they were starting to understand that it wasn't something only 'geeks' did, but in fact something they did all the time and would continue to do long after they were qualified.

The second class - a reflection

Reflecting on this aspect of my teaching; the use of pictures and images, made me plan something new for the second action research lesson. My use of the image that illustrated the course with the year two modules added seemed to have been well received. I'd used this same approach periodically over the previous year and so it was familiar to the students; they almost expected it. When I casually asked them, while packing away at the end of the first lesson, if any of them had tried something like this to put their course into a 'visual context', they all said no. When pressed, they all acknowledged the worth of such a tool, but when it came to having a go themselves they said things like '*I can't draw*', '*I'm not very artistic*', or '*I've never been creative*'. This makes me question whether it would be interesting to set an assessed piece of work that required them to do something like this within their own practice. Clearly it would need a verbal explanation, but I feel that if they could distil their ideas into a picture or visual representation, it may help their clarity of mind. Many students have difficulty with new ideas which are almost always described using words and texts and as my initial teacher training companion (Petty, 2006: 113) so rightly says of these methods:

> ...[they] cannot contain all the detail, so the learner is forced to isolate the key points and their relations. To see the wood for the trees.

So if we can help them to make sense of these things through a medium other than words this may have an advantage for some trainees.

These reflections had made me re-think my planning for the next lesson. The class entitled; 'The Action Research Journey,' involves showing the students the basic chronological steps to be taken within this module. For this I normally present the steps to the students on a PowerPoint slide, with key headings, followed by a paired activity. Each pair is given an envelope with cards inside. Some cards have these same key headings written on them, plus there are lots of other cards with more detailed points relating to the action research journey and each one relates in some way to one of the key headings. In pairs, the students find the cards with the key headings, set these out in chronological order (as shown on my slide, Figure 3) and then try to match the rest of the cards to the correct heading.

Identify and Justify Research Action	• An idea to be explored. • A teaching and learning problem. • Ideally value - based. • Supported by theory/other research.
Identify Research Question	• State what it is hoped will be achieved with whom and why. • Often stated as questions: 'In doing X, how will students respond?'
Set Out a Research Design	• Appropriate to the collection, sorting and identifying of data identified. • Issues of triangulation identified. • Potential problems and ethical issues considered.
Embark on the Research and Gather Data	• Respond to unforeseen circumstances. • Watch for bias and acknowledge the researchers' central role. • Collect, sort, code and present data.
Generate Evidence from Data	• Interpret data. • Explore relationship to research questions.
Make a Claim to Knowledge	• Show what new knowledge/understanding has been generated. • Detail new questions that might have emerged.

(Figure 3)

What I decided to do, in addition to this and based upon my reflections, was to produce my own hand-drawn pictures representing key points in the research journey. I made them roughly A5 in size, laminated them and intended to use them as a formative test at the start of the third class, to see how it affected the students' recall of the action research journey they'd just laid out in words using my cards. In the event, it didn't happen like this.

I briefly presented the students with the key headings for the research journey, gave out the envelopes with the cards in them, paired them up and sat back to watch how they got on deciphering the words and phrases on the cards and then finally selecting the key heading under which each one should go. I saw that one pair, the two PGCE students who often sit with one another, had raced through the exercise whilst the others were still grappling with a number of the cards. Surprisingly this pair had got a few of the cards in the wrong place and having had this pointed out to them, they continued.

When the matching exercise ended, I noted that some of the trainees had resorted to just guessing which card went where and I overheard one of them say '*just put that card there. That heading only has one card and it all looks out of balance*'. Meanwhile the two students who had finished and correctly placed all the cards looked rather pleased with their efforts. The others, while they'd made a reasonable attempt, had got bored rather more quickly and had resorted to placing cards based on the overall visual balance of all the cards and not on what they actually said. We went over their results and once we'd discussed these I had an urge to use my pictures there and then as an immediate follow up to the matching exercise.

The 'symmetry' of this idea seemed just the right thing to do. Use words for one exercise and immediately follow it up with the same activity, more or less, but using pictures, and see what happens. I asked the pairs to leave the cards they'd just matched on their desks. I gave them the packs of pictures with blu-tac and told them to stick the pictures up on the walls behind them. Then using the cards they'd left behind on their desks as reference, try to identify which picture represented which card and to then place the pictures in the correct chronological order and stick the card from the earlier activity that they thought the image represented alongside the image, like a heading. The end result would be a visual representation of 'The Research Journey' with titles taken from the original matching exercise. The image and heading are illustrated below in Figure 4.

1. A teaching and learning problem, or an idea to be explored

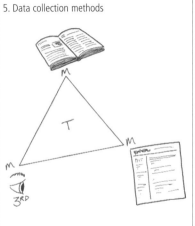

or

2. Value based

V

3. Supported by theory

T

4. Identify research questions

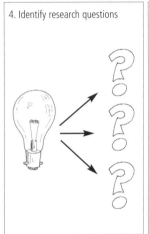

5. Data collection methods

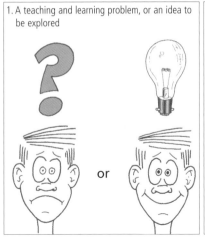

6. Collect, sort and code data

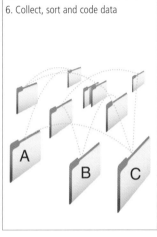

A   B   C

7. Present data

8. Explore relationships to research questions

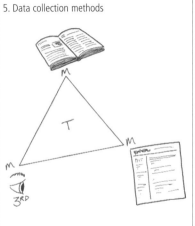

9. Detail new questions that might emerge

this way?
this way?
this way?

What occurred proved quite inspiring and became one of those, 'this is why I teach' moments. My impulsive reaction to my students' response to the card exercise and the fact I had a resource prepared for the following week in front of me at that moment led to something totally unplanned but, much more meaningful than what I'd thought to do next. In brief, the trainees who struggled with the first task and ended up guessing loved the exercise. The pictures seemed to make the words written on the cards more meaningful for them. They engaged with the activity with a renewed energy and enthusiasm and most importantly with great success, often interpreting the images correctly in seconds. The two trainees who were successful on the first task on the other hand were now struggling. The contrast between their successes with the words on the cards and this visual challenge was quite something to behold. In particular, one student became visibly stressed and quite hot and bothered. She and her partner, both graduates, kept saying how difficult they were finding it, how silly this exercise was and were in general experiencing something truly unpleasant for them. By the time the other students, who were vocational teachers, had finished with some success, they found themselves mired in confusion with some pictures pinned up, some on the floor, and others still on their desk with the cards from the previous exercise, scattered and out of order.

When the exercise ended, after 10 or so minutes, the contrast between the students was quite evident. One set of students, now able to complete the task, were 'buzzing' with the previously successful pair having to sit down in frustration, amazed at their inability to make sense of the pictures. The pictorial successful pairs presented their results, describing with real insight the meaning of the images as they saw it and in so doing, started to show a real understanding of the research journey and its nature. Throughout their presentations and the subsequent discussions, the pictorial unsuccessful pair kept saying '*I just don't think like that*', '*how did you get that from that image?*' and '*I can see it now that it's explained, but I just couldn't get my mind to translate the pictures - give me a book any day!*'

I abandoned the rest of the class. There was about an hour left and the discussion that followed, largely led by the students, was a moment that truly inspired me. These contrasting reactions to the pictures acted like a catalyst to a discussion that if filmed, could have made for a useful addition to the student's portfolios, if not a gradable summative assessment. In reflecting on 'what just happened?', we discussed learning styles, in particular Holists and Serialists, past educational experiences and their effect on future learning, the contrast between vocational and academic educational histories, the possible use of pictures and images as nationally recognised summative assessment tools as opposed to written exams and assignments. In fact issues related to teaching and learning that I'd never covered in previous classes emerged. Students became critical reflectors for that hour. Their egos and potential embarrassments were put to one side, enabling them to engage in a meaningful professional discussion about their practice and what all this might mean to them and to their learners. I loved it and I think they did too. In fact we were thrown out by estates staff because we ran over for so long.

The learning was not restricted to that hour and a half either as the student who got most stressed by the picture activity came to say that she had abandoned her initial action research idea for an examination of how using pictures and images in her teaching would affect her practice and development and her students' learning. I thought action research really isn't for geeks once you can see the whole picture.

Conclusion

I've decided after re-reading what I've just written and consulting with my colleagues putting this publication together, that the only fit and proper way to complete the reflective cycle of this chapter is to send a draft to one of the students who, when I used the images in my last class, found things very difficult. In fact this is the student who, despite being academically gifted, was most challenged by the exercise and appeared to get visibly stressed. Moreover, this is also the student who after reflecting on the experience herself, decided to change her action research idea and is now in the middle of exploring how the use of images in her teaching may impact on her learners and indeed her own teaching practice.

It is to Christine's eternal credit that she took an apparently negative learning experience and largely unprompted by me, decided to turn it into a way of positively challenging her own teaching for the good of her learners. It is decisions like this, that your trainees make once in a while, that truly remind you of 'why we do this'.

We had arranged a tutorial to discuss her action research project. I emailed her the draft of this piece and asked if she could come in an hour or so earlier to discuss what I'd written, as I would value her feedback. Thankfully she agreed and at the allotted time we sat down in my office to discuss her thoughts on it.

What surprised me most was my nervousness. I wanted her to 'like' the piece and respond positively. This made me think about how our own students must feel. They frequently send in drafts of their work and a few days later come in to discuss it. I hadn't quite appreciated the feelings of anticipation and anxiousness that must precipitate this process. Giving them feedback on their work is something I just do, with little thought. After this experience, I will be somewhat more sympathetic.

Our discussions proved highly illuminating. Christine said how much she'd enjoyed reading the piece and how it had brought back the memories of the class and her feelings of frustration. But what was most heartening was that she said reading the piece had 'renewed' her interest in her own action research. I was aware that, for students carrying out the action research module, the journey is never a smooth one and enthusiasm and motivation must ebb and flow. I was delighted to think that my musings in this chapter had rekindled her interest in doing her own project - not least because I feel I have an additional vested interest in her efforts. In a way the experiences explored in this chapter is a precursor to her research, which seems to add to my hopes for her work - so no pressure there, Christine!

Reading my draft also reminded her of the discussions that followed my class. She remembered asking one of her classmates at the time '*is this how you feel when you're given an essay to do?*' To which the answer was an emphatic '*yes!*' The experience had given her a true taste of how so many learners must feel when faced with what they perceive to be an 'academic' and wordy assessment. Because of Christine's background as a historian and archivist, the essay writing process and the use of words to express learning, are 'normal'. Their potential to strike fear into learners without her sort of background, hadn't quite been appreciated. My class and the use of images had given her a vivid insight into this and it was heartening to hear her modest and honest reflections on this. She went on to say how she thought it was important to tell her classmate how '*useless*' she had felt when trying to do my exercise. This was quite interesting, as it now makes me appreciate how self-conscious Christine must have felt at times, believing she was perceived as the 'clever, academic one' in the class; a perception that may have made her feel marginalised at times. It's salutary to think how I hadn't really picked up on this when taking the class.

The element of our discussions that I found most illuminating and with which I want to end this piece, is to do with Christine's comments on how interesting it had been getting an insight into my thoughts as her teacher training tutor. She hadn't realised the extent to which I consciously or unconsciously consider them as learners, adjusting my planning and my teaching strategies to suit and sometimes, as in the case of this class, how I spontaneously change things, because my instinct tells me that something might happen that could be educationally positive and meaningful. She was aware that I try to 'model' good practice when teaching the class and often have mid-class 'time-outs', to discuss how I've just taught something. But the nature and process of this had only now become apparent to her, having been given this chapter to read.

I thought this was a fascinating observation and we began to talk about how interesting it would be, for us as teacher training tutors, to share with our learners, the sort of reflections I've explored in this chapter. Almost, a parallel 'tutor journal', made available to our learners at important points throughout the course, to give an alternative perspective on what we hope they're learning at that moment. After all, as tutors, we ask our teacher training students to reflect in a professional journal throughout their course. We tell them how important and useful this process is to their development as teachers and how when we periodically read snippets of what they write, it often gives us a vivid 'window' into their thinking as trainee teachers. So, could it work the other way round? Tutors could update a reflective blog that students could have remote access to. The reflections could coincide with particular elements of the curriculum, including assessments, or in response to interesting situations or discussions that may have ensued in a class. This would allow students to engage with the reflective process that we all should be going through, as a fellow teacher, not so much as a student. It would also give us, as teacher training tutors an opportunity to model practice that could inspire and perhaps motivate, much as Christine's motivation to do her action research was rekindled somewhat by reading this chapter. Indeed students could respond to the reflections and add their own thoughts, much as Christine has with me.

I feel this process, if carefully managed and entered into by all, in a spirit of collaboration, support and professional development might prove illuminating. We might learn a great deal about the student/teacher relationship. I should try this with my full time PGCE students next year - naturally, I'd start by drawing a visual representation of the process; '*a glimpse of the whole at a glance*' (Black, 2002: 3), just to see what might happen and what I might learn.

References

Black, A. (2002) *Making Sense of What it Means to Teach: Artful Representations as Meaning Making Tools*, Volume 6 (Number 1).

Petty, G. (2006) *Evidence Based Teaching: A Practical Approach*. Cheltenham: Nelson.

'You have to be in it to win it': Reflections on action research

Karen Kay

Introduction

For the past five years, I have been working as a teacher educator in a further education (FE) college, which provides substantial higher education (HE) provision, as well as a diverse variety of FE courses. We offer teaching qualifications to a wide range of vocational and non-vocational tutors, these teachers delivering subjects in both the FE and HE sectors. Recent course changes have resulted in the need for these practitioners to undertake an action research project in the second half of their Certificate or Post Graduate Certificate in Education (Cert Ed/ PGCE).

The purpose of this chapter is to provide an insight for those readers who may be interested in attempting their own action research study, or for those who support action researchers in some way. The aim of this chapter therefore, is to inspire any practitioner who may be considering an action research module either as part of a teaching qualification, their everyday practice or as a method for creating meaningful Continuing Professional Development (CPD). It could also be illuminating for teacher educators who may be asked to guide and support tutors undertaking action research for the first time. The chapter examines the hopes and fears of twelve novice researchers and tracks their journeys from the inception of thinking about possible research interventions through to the completion, (in most cases), of their project. It describes their thoughts and feelings, and how their projects have transpired, whilst individuals disclose frankly and honestly, the difficulties that they have encountered and the benefits that they may have enjoyed through completion of their individual studies. These professionals also importantly go on to offer some candid advice to those who may be about to embark on their own journey of research discovery.

I have also included reflections outlining my own journey whilst supporting these trainee teachers so that I can examine and improve my own teaching provision and the support offered for future trainee teachers embarking on a similar path. I would like to take this opportunity to thank these participants who have so openly agreed to share their research pathways so that others may learn from their experiences.

The group of participants that this study is based on are predominantly vocational trainee teachers and of the group, ten are on the Cert Ed and two on the PGCE programme. This was to be their first venture into practitioner-led research and their initial fears, concerns and trepidations have caused great personal reflection both for these tutors and myself. Many of them would be at great pains to explain that they had never had to tackle anything remotely like this level of formalised research before, either at school, (at university for the two PGCE learners), or subsequently in their respective industries or teaching careers.

These trainee teachers initially found the requirements of this module both daunting and bewildering; I can clearly remember the stunned silence from this usually vocal and vibrant group when they were initially told of the action research unit's learning outcomes. Yet as ever, I have been struck again and again by the enthusiasm, dedication and professionalism of these trainee teachers, many of whom are part-time and relatively new to teaching. Yet they are frequently tasked to motivate and engage learners who may enter college with low levels of self-esteem, or who struggle financially to further their education, due to the levels of deprivation in several of the boroughs in the local area. It is these trainee teachers' passion for their subject and the handing over of this knowledge to equip their learners with a mixture of life and professional skills, that brings them to teaching, and it is that same passion that has led them to wanting to take part in this study so that other teachers may learn from their experiences of the action research process.

Action research has grown in importance and stature in both the educational and social welfare sectors, so that now in the United Kingdom, many educational and social policy initiatives feature a practitioner-research element amongst their key requirements, [For a discussion of this see, for example: Davies *et al*. (2007)]. This type of self-reflective enquiry whereby the practitioner, in this case the teaching professional, sets out to conduct a line of research that is closely linked to enhancing their own personal practice, helps to ensure that the research is relevant to the practitioner. The researcher arguably therefore, feels a greater sense of ownership and commitment to the project and to any practice or policy changes that result from their research conclusions. This growth in practitioner-led research and its implications for the improvement of professional practice also means that the senior management of many organisations are increasingly recognising its power, becoming more engaged in the research process and its outcomes. It is for these reasons that an action research module has been introduced into the teaching qualification that we offer.

The twelve research - practitioners

Five of the participants have been teaching for less than two years, three of these as part-time trainee teachers. Five participants have been teaching between two to four years, and of these two are again working as part-time trainee teachers. The remaining two respondents have been teaching full-time for eight and ten years respectively.

Specialist subject areas of these trainee teachers are predominantly vocational in nature. The specialist subjects are: three teaching NVQ Hairdressing Levels 1-3; three teaching NVQ Beauty Therapy Levels 1-3; one NVQ Painting and Decorating Levels 1-3; one teaching City and Guilds Veterinary Nursing, two, teaching Phlebotomy and Parent Education in the NHS respectively, one teaching French at A and AS Levels and one teaching literacy and numeracy for adult males in one of Her Majesty's institutions. The age range of learners that they teach is predominantly from fourteen to nineteen years of age, with only three of the twelve experiencing learner groups where the minimum age is twenty years and above.

The planned timescale of the intervention in most cases, (eight out of twelve), was up to two months, with four interventions planned to take between two and four months. All of the participants had planned and collected at least three types of data to allow for more rigorous triangulation so that their findings would be more valid and reliable. Data was collected from a variety of methods including questionnaires, formal and informal interviews, observations, measurement of irrelevant interruptions to the lesson noting where and with whom learners naturally chose to sit in practical sessions and the measurement of predicted and achieved test and assignment results.

Findings of the study

Initial trepidations and fears

Common to all of the trainee teachers was a feeling that this was something that they were not equipped to deal with, as one person put it *'Everything was daunting at first'*. This was from a trainee teacher who had consistently demonstrated a very high standard of practical teaching and written academic assignments. A second trainee teacher also used the word *'daunting'* adding that they felt ill-equipped to analyse the data. A third stated that they were *'overwhelmed'*. Yet another trainee teacher said that they were uneasy *'about the unknown and nervous if it would work?'*

Similarly a trainee teacher initially said that she was *'Very unsure how to go about the intervention and quite negative as to whether any intervention would work'*. Another stated that *'I was unsure of action research and whether it would have any impact'*.

All the trainee teachers struggled initially with the concept of this type of research, saying *'I didn't really understand the concept of action research'*, or *'I was very unsure how to go about finding research and finding an intervention'*. Another stated that they were *'completely overwhelmed and didn't understand what was expected'*. It should be noted that two months into the intervention to support mature learners with dyslexia, this same teacher now feels that feedback from the learners has already been very positive and the amount of measured improvement has been sufficient for the intervention to be formalised in future policy procedures at the organisation in which she works. In fact she feels, *'…so enthused that I want to publish!'*

Other common concerns were that the research process would be extremely time consuming and at an academic standard that was out of reach. One trainee teacher wondered *'how are you going to fit it in over the time, with the other lessons?'* These points are summed up by one graduate trainee teacher who has taught adults for over eight years who felt that *'I don't have the time'*…and the exercise is *'very academic'*, fearful that it would be at a level which would prove unobtainable for her.

Strong initial fears and concerns were indeed expressed by eleven of the twelve trainee teachers taking part in this study. Only one was positive at the onset saying *'I felt it would be interesting to try and it would help to develop my own teaching'*.

Aims of interventions

Intervention aims for the twelve trainee teachers were varied and diverse. Three were targeted to improve group work or group dynamics within a practical environment or a more formal class room situation. Two were concerned with the increased motivation of learners, the first being a consideration of how to keep individuals motivated in theory classes as part of a vocational subject. The other was targeted at how to motivate learners who were at differing levels of achievement and ability in a large class size.

Two of the other projects were about improving time-management either of the learners so that they could prioritise their time effectively, or by reducing the number of irrelevant interruptions in the session each week. Two other studies involved developing learners' written and spoken language abilities and another two concerned improvement of practical skills so that learners were either more aware of their own and others' body language in a client- consultant situation or how to improve on practical techniques when delivering beauty treatments. The last intervention was to keep staff updated with new theory and practical techniques in a vocational-medical setting.

Difficulties

Learner co-operation

Interestingly the most commonly expressed difficulty that researchers thought would be problematic at the start was not identifying the intervention itself but, gaining the co-operation of the learners. Eight trainee teachers expressed concerns about the co-operation of the learner-group. For example: *'Knowing if the students would be enthusiastic to be involved'*, and *'...implementing the intervention, how would it be received by the learners and would it work?'* Trainee teachers seemed, after careful consideration, to be able to highlight a problem that might be improved by a process and used their gut feelings, professional experience and reflections through instruments such as professional development journals, to narrow down to a specific aim.

Data collection and analysis

The second most common envisaged and encountered difficulty was choosing and designing methods of data collection. Seven of the participants expressed major problems in this area. To illustrate this, a comment from one researcher was *'Thinking of the problem and what methods to use to get the best results'*. Others found that *'The design of questionnaires proved difficult'*, or that *'wording the questionnaire'*, and *'developing a questionnaire'*, were the main problems in this area. Two practitioners found that their initial questionnaires did not give sufficient data so that *'questions were not completed fully'*. Both of these trainees subsequently found that they had to rethink their initial questionnaire format because of this and would consider a pilot questionnaire when undertaking further research studies.

Three trainees stressed problems with analysing and presenting the data once collected. One commented on the difficulty of *'Thinking of what evidence to use in a specific way'*, whilst another stated that it was going to be difficult *'to transfer findings into an academic essay'*.

Time constraints

Four trainee teachers also cited time constraints as a major cause for concern and worried how they would fit in observations and interviews into lessons, as these would cause time pressures within an already tight curriculum. Others questioned where they would find the additional time needed on top of normal teaching duties to interview learners and to undertake other data collection methods and analyses.

Easiest to achieve

Towards the end of most of the interventions, participants were asked what they had found easiest to achieve and whether their feelings and attitudes had changed from the initial phase of their project. All bar one of the respondents felt more positive about their studies in the areas that follow.

Identifying the aim of the intervention

Five of the practitioners thought that setting up the intervention once the aim had been decided upon was the least problematical aspect of their action research. One commented for example *'Once I had decided on the intervention, it came quite easily!'* A second trainee said that *'Deciding on the intervention idea and then setting it up'* was the easiest aspect and a third stated that *'setting up the initial problem'*, was the simplest to achieve.

Researching and writing up the research

Four of the practitioners found that the research and writing of their study was the least difficult. One said that it was *'the writing up by breaking into pieces'*, which was the least difficult, whilst three others found that action research theory was quite readily available from a variety of sources. This is an interesting finding as many stated this as a fear at the beginning particularly about writing at what they saw as the right academic level.

Creation of questionnaires

Three of the participants found that the design and data collection method of using questionnaires was the easiest and quickest way to obtain meaningful data. They were pleased with the richness of data they could collect from questionnaires that included a mixture of quantitative questions such as tick boxes and qualitative open questions that asked for learner feedback and opinions. Slightly more participants found this less easy.

Advice to other researchers

Many of the twelve researcher-practitioners gave similar comments when asked what advice each would give to someone who was about to embark on an action research study. Two clear themes emerged:

• Plan early and don't panic!

Eight trainee teachers said that it was important to start planning early with careful consideration of what results were achievable. They suggested it was important not to panic or to rush the intervention, but to have faith in their initial reflections and feelings, whilst also keeping an open mind.

• The KISS principle.

The other four trainee teachers advocated advice that was summed up by one person as, 'The KISS principle - Keep Idea Simple and Specific'. These practitioners all outlined the importance of not taking on too big a problem, and to avoid over-complication of aims and objectives.

Benefits from the interventions

The range of benefits expressed by these practitioners was varied, both in the degree of analysed success and the area that had been improved upon, this being dependent on the specific nature and aim of each individual's research. The majority were pleased that their intervention had resulted in specific ways to enhance their own teaching practice so that for example, improvements in learning achievement and retention of their learners could be detected. The twelve researchers found that the benefits were, through the nature of the action research process, clearly linked to their own personal professional practice, whatever the context of their teaching, and these teaching professionals frequently talked in terms of an increasing level of confidence in their own professional competencies. Many found that this research process also increased their motivation to reflect and act on aspects of their teaching in the future, having in this instance successfully chosen, designed, implemented and analysed their own research project.

At this time not all of the interventions have been completed. However, eight of the twelve researcher-practitioners have already described seeing some positive improvement in the teaching and learning situation that they had set out to improve. Of the remaining four, two have also detected slight changes so far.

One trainee teacher in a vocational setting, had experiences of learners who struggled to time-manage written coursework and practical work effectively. Her intervention, where learners have been given individual support to set their own short, medium, and long term goals and aspirations, has delivered additional benefits as well as the hopeful improvement of time-management skills. Although incomplete, the intervention seems to be resulting in learners 'managing their time better' when in class, with the additional benefits of 'completing their homework on time' and 'improving motivation' of the learners. This is expected to lead to anticipated higher standards of generated coursework evidence. This is a formidable list of improvements from one relatively short-term research project.

Another trainee teacher, who has just started a full-time Beauty Therapy post, decided on an intervention where learners would be given access to a series of practical demonstrations which were put onto the College's Virtual Learning Environment, (VLE). That way they could be accessed at any time by the learners via the Internet. Again, although this project has not yet been completed, positive feedback has been such from both the learners and course tutors, that this access may well be extended and formalised as part of the institution's future ICT policy as learners have been able to understand and carry out complex practical treatments in a shorter period of time.

Other improvements detected so far in various interventions have included increased levels of learner interaction and engagement, improved group dynamics and reduced occurrence of learner cliques. Another benefit that has been identified by some of the participating trainees has been that intervention ideas have been greeted with interest by other teaching colleagues with at least two departmental managers already stating that they will incorporate the intervention into policy for appropriate faculty areas if it transpires that the conclusions are as positive as they appear to be thus far. This has raised the visibility and professional standing of these individuals within their department and organisation, and both seem excited about their newly acquired status and confidence in research.

Reflections

The purpose of this chapter has been to provide an insight for those readers who may be interested in attempting their own action research study, or for those who support action researchers in some way. It is not meant to be a comprehensive list of the history and key theorists in action research development [For more detailed accounts, see Noffke (1997a) and Carr and Kemmis (1986)], nor has it been written up as a piece of action research in its own right, although indeed it could have been. However, the study did transpire to become an action research project. I have therefore purposely not expanded on the data collection methods and the triangulation used to collect and collate this data, [For those interested in the subject of triangulation to ensure reliability and validity, sources could include Denscombe (2002: 134), Kane and O'Reilly-de Brun (2001: 145), Gorard and Taylor (2004: 44) and Cohen *et al.* (2007: 141)]. Suffice it to say that the methodology, data collection methods and potential ethical issues were carefully considered resulting in an intervention design which included data collection via a mixture of questionnaires, open individual interviews, group discussions and marked, draft and finished assignments.

In this study, eleven of the twelve participants initially felt ill at ease when asked to undertake an action research project and these feelings included being extremely overwhelmed and daunted. These results would strongly suggest that many FE teachers, and in this case many vocational FE teachers, have not primarily encountered research in its empirical form and as such have viewed it as something for scientists and university professors to pursue and use - not something that would be of use to them in their own individual teaching practice. This was particularly true for the vocational teachers in this study, and it is something for which these practitioners felt ill-equipped to use or for which traditionally, they have perceived little value or place in their own educational practice and professional development. However, of the twelve professionals in the study, all bar one, felt positive about the process having participated in action research for the first time and they generally expressed noticeable improvements in the situation that each had set out to tackle in their intervention. (It should be noted that the twelfth tutor who did not enjoy any aspect of the research, did see a marked decrease in the amount of irrelevant lesson interruptions in their classes and so arguably achieved some benefit from the intervention).

Action research is by necessity an extension of reflective practice, Schön (1983, 1995), and is therefore often referred to as practitioner-led research. Ultimately it is the practitioner who is the researcher and this form of research allows a self-analysis of what can be improved, with the practitioner then taking action and subsequently providing evidence to show how the action has improved the situation, (McNiff and Whitehead, 2002). It quickly became evident that these practitioners, part way through their own individual research processes, began to feel empowered and more confident in their own professional abilities so that through formalised reflection, they could identify the initial aim and intervention. Indeed, deciding on an intervention was the factor that the largest proportion of these participants thought to be the least difficult part of their research project.

All of the participants in this study realised the need for rigorous data collection methods to allow triangulation, and open-minded data analysis, so that their results could be substantiated and strongly defended. It is this rigour that allows the practitioner to feel confident in the benefits that they have gained from their intervention so that their findings will stand up to close scrutiny and may well help to enhance both the confidence and professional standing of the researcher-practitioner in their teaching environment as some of these tutors have already found.

It is essential that researchers should be, as Bell and Opie succinctly say: '...*constantly on the lookout for signs of bias...placing great emphasis on reflection on practice and on triangulation*' (Bell and Opie, 2002: 129). From the comments and practice of these trainee teachers, it is important if not vital, for the researcher to keep an open mind when collecting and analysing their data. As Child states: '*How unbiased can research be? The act of choosing a subject for research nearly always reflects a bias*' (Child, 2004: 335).

It is therefore imperative that as action researchers we design studies that include rigorous triangulation when deciding on data collection methods. For example Denscombe (2002: 13) emphasises that perfect research is unattainable and a researcher '*cannot please all the people all the time*', but careful awareness of important research ground rules of data collection methods should allow results that can be defended and justified, whilst potentially being relevant and beneficial to a varied audience.

The practitioners in this study often found questionnaires to be the quickest way to obtain data. This is not surprising as they are a popular and commonly used method, although unsurprisingly, several found that successful design was crucial to provide rich and meaningful data and more informatively, a pilot questionnaire could help minimise mistakes early in the data collection cycle. Several of the researchers concluded that to be of the most benefit their research should be as Denscombe (2002: 12) suggests '*on time and in time*'. The action research approach can prove to be a very important form of practitioner research, and is largely as these twelve practitioners would concur '*enquiry conducted by the self into the self*' (McNiff, 2002: 15). Reflection is a central part of this process:

> *Action research is a form of collective self-reflective enquiry undertaken by participants in social situations in order to improve the rationality and justice of their own social or educational practices, as well as their understanding of those practices, and the situations in which the practices are carried out.*

> (Kemmis and McTaggart, 1988: 5-6)

Action research originally came to prominence within the teaching profession with Kurt Lewin being widely recognised as its pioneer developing an early action research theory, which is generally known as the action-reflection cycle of planning, acting, observing and reflecting (Lewin, 1946). It's initial growth slowed until theorists such as Kemmis (1993) and Elliott (1991) championed the benefits of action research again. Both extended Lewin's work to portray action research as a self-reflective spiral to improve chosen aspects of the researcher- practitioner's educational practice. I would suggest that this form of research can offer us this evolving spiral of improved professional practice with the resulting delivery of more effective teaching and support for our learners. It was also via this challenging, but rewarding, process of cyclical self-reflection that these twelve practitioners aspired to identify then act on a specific teaching problem that might benefit from intervention through observing any changes in the situation before reflecting upon that situation again.

Many key theorists such as Stringer (1999) would agree that there are three distinct phases to the action research process, namely:

Look - Where we define and describe the problem to be investigated and the context in which it is set.

Think - Where we interpret and explain. Are any problems or issues evident?

Act - Where we try to resolve those detected issues and problems.

The twelve research-practitioners discussed here, all followed these steps diligently and thoughtfully, whilst during this study, I have also undergone these same phases. Initially, I encountered both reticence and confusion from these trainee teachers when considering action research, and I have subsequently collected and collated common themes from the study data so that their perceived issues and problems with the action research process would become evident. The last phase has not reached a full resolution, but conclusions from the study including tips and advice from these twelve researchers to future researchers on how to undertake similar projects, may well prove illuminating and I hope that the process of writing this article may help those looking to embark on similar research journeys, so that other novice action researchers decide to undertake projects that grow to provide benefits to both their learners and themselves.

In agreement with Davies *et al.* (2007), action research should not be something that is detached from a teacher's day-to-day work issues, but is indeed something which can greatly enhance day-to-day and longer term problems encountered in their professional practice. The action research journey, should not be taken lightly, and can be a difficult and emotional path, as some of the comments and observations from these participants have indicated, but it can also be life-enhancing and empowering for the researcher-practitioner. Several members of this group commented on their increase in professional confidence and were generally enthused by the range of benefits and improvements that they had measured. Having performed this particular action research process myself, I can now hope to empathise more with my learners and to ultimately offer more intuitive and empathic support for future cohorts of teacher education students. Like other contributors to this book, I have found that it can be the case that an individual researcher may be too close to a problem themselves to see and plan their intervention and data collection methods clearly. Certainly these researcher-practitioners have found that the ideas, discussion and support from peers within their group, have helped to clarify what steps they could take to simplify the aim of their research and how to choose and design data collection tools that allow effective measurement pre and post-intervention.

As a group of teacher-practitioners, we have generally found this research process to be *'equitable'* as a means of *'acknowledging people's equality of worth'* (Stringer, 1999: 9), so that new student teachers and longer established teachers alike, can undertake interventions that not only have the potential for improving their own teaching situations and professional development, but may also have far-reaching implications for a wider professional audience. This process has also certainly been *'democratic, enabling the participation of all people'* (p 10), for both the researcher-practitioner and their learners, and several practitioners have found it to be *'liberating, providing freedom from oppressive, debilitating conditions'* (p 10).

Although this form of research frequently focuses on individual practitioner's practice, action research may also offer wider implications for senior management within the practitioner's organisation, or potentially even farther afield through achieving improvements in learner achievement and retention as seen in many of the interventions outlined here. As the practitioner's research aims are primarily to improve some aspect of teaching and learning within their organisation, a management structure that positively encourages action research by, for example, releasing the teacher from some of their other duties, and one which disseminates the results of the practitioner research throughout the establishment, will be an organisational environment in which staff are more likely to undertake this type of project enthusiastically and diligently. [A discussion of how the impact of practitioner research can be maximised and advice on how practitioners should get started, maintain momentum and publish and disseminate their findings can be found in Davies *et al.* (2007)].

In conclusion, enquiry and critical and open reflection, is part of what we as teaching professionals do. Action research provides a way to formalise this process whereby practitioners can initiate interventions to improve their practice with this type of practitioner-led research having the potential to offer diverse and wide-reaching benefits for both practitioner and organisation alike. We as teaching professionals may well view action research as an aspect of teaching practice that we would be ill-advised to ignore, for as summarised in that well-known catchphrase of the UK's National Lottery slogan: *'You have to be in it to win it!'* (www.bbc.co.uk/lottery).

References

Bell, J. and Opie, C. (2002) *Learning from research: Getting more from your data*. Buckingham: Open University Press.

Carr, W. and Kemmis, S. (1986) *Becoming Critical: Education, Knowledge and Action Research*. London: Falmer.

Child, D. (2004) *Psychology and the teacher*. London: Continuum.

Cohen, L., Manion, L. and Morrison, K. (2007) *Research methods in education*, (6th edn). Abingdon: Routledge.

Davies, P., Hamilton, M. and James, K. (2007) *Maximising the impact of practitioner research. A handbook of practical advice*. London: NRDC.

Denscombe, M. (2002) *Ground Rules for Good Research a 10 point guide for social researchers*. Maidenhead: Open University Press.

Elliott, J. (1991) *Action Research for Educational Change*. Buckingham: Open University Press.

Gorard, S. and Taylor, C. (2004) *Combining Methods in Educational and Social Research*. New York: Open University Press.

Kane, E. and O'Reilly-de Brun, M. (2001) *Doing your own research*. London: Marion Boyars Publishers.

Kemmis, S. (1993) Action Research, in: M. Hammersley (Ed.), *Educational Research: Current Issues*. London: Open University Press.

Kemmis, S. and McTaggart, R. (1988) *The Action Research Planner*, (3rd edn). Geelong: Deakin University Press.

Lewin, K. (1946) *Action Research and minority problems. Journal of Social Issues*. 2(4): pp 34-46.

McNiff, J. and Whitehead, J. (2002) *Action Research Principles and Practice*, (2nd edn). Oxon: RoutledgeFalmer.

Noffke, S. (1997a) Themes and tensions in US action research: Towards historical analysis. S. Hollingworth (Ed.), *International Action Research: A Casebook for Educational Reform*. London: Falmer.

Schön, D. (1983) *The Reflective Practitioner: How Professionals Think in Action*. New York: Basic Books.

Schön, D. (1995) Knowing-in-action: The new scholarship requires a new epistemology. *Change* November-December. pp 27-34.

Stringer, E. T. (1999) *Action Research*: London: Sage Publications.

The National Lottery. Results January 24th 2009. < *www.bbc.co.uk/lottery/*> Accessed 24/01/09.

Mentoring: A tool for learning, reflection and action

Alex Pandolfo

Introduction

I have been involved in learning and ways of learning since 1975 when I was involved in Trade Union Education. The Trade Union Education provision put the emphasis on the learner and the process of learning from experience. Currently I work in a further education (FE) college in Cumbria teaching on the Certificate/ Post Graduate Certificate in Education (Cert Ed/PGCE), the BA (Hons) in Education and Continuing Professional Development (CPD) programmes. I still, in a much more informed way, advocate a learner-centred, process-based learning experience which I develop through reflective practice and continued action research.

I wish to say at this stage that I do not see action research as an academic activity governed by academic rules but as an integral aspect of my practice. I believe that the most effective action research is not recorded in chapters, journals or assignments but in personal journals and the evaluation section of lesson plans a much undervalued aspect of lesson plans that appears to be ignored by many organisations and validating bodies when conducting classroom observations. I ask you to interpret any reference to reflection and action research as part of my everyday activity of reflecting and acting in and on action. I locate reflection and action at the centre of all my unique learning experience (teaching).

This chapter attempts to demonstrate how I have learnt from reflection, action research and my learners. It also puts forward the argument that a process based mentoring system provided by a subject specialist aids the mentor and the mentee to be involved in a continuing learning spiral. It supports personal learning and development and provides a deeper learning and quality based experience for our learners. This approach endorses the argument '*Whoever learns together, grows together*' (Klasen and Clutterbuck, 2002: 18). I also suggest that a subject process based mentoring system located in initial teacher training (ITT) can embed the principles of reflective practice, promote the ideas and practice of action research and support the ethos of CPD. In this way mentoring as a tool for learning becomes an integral aspect of learning by developing reflective practice (Schön, 1991). It can also develop critical thought (Foucault, 1987), autonomy of learning, participation and action (McNiff *et al.*, 2003) and is committed to educational improvement.

Finally this reflects my subjective perspective developed through personal continuous reflective practice, personal learning, and action research. Accordingly I use the '*personal pronoun I*' (Creswell 1998.16) to celebrate and acknowledge my subjectivity, role and involvement in this discourse. The use of the word discourse will be interpreted as argued by (Foucault, 1987; Dreyfus and Rabinow, 1982; Smith and Pandolfo, 2003) to include all spoken words, actions, and our personal contextualised perspective present in the discursive practices of learning. I have, and will continue to reflect on '*how I fit into my research, how I influence wider social context*' (McNiff *et al.*, 2003: 20-21) and the impact of this to my practice.

Monitoring practice and gathering data

This piece of work discusses action research (my practice) carried out in February 2007 as part of my daily practice whilst teaching sessions on action research with a full time Cert Ed/ PGCE group. It was clear that I was not meeting the needs of the group despite continuous reflection, discussions with my colleague and using a wide range of teaching styles and methods. Whilst preparing for the action research and during it I attempted to draw on a feminist approach that included being collaborative, being non - exploitative, avoiding the objectification of participants and for the outcome to be transformative. I discussed with the group that I wished to conduct the research and that we could use it to bring about changes to my practice, enhance their learning, and model action research. Data was collected initially through the use of a standard course evaluation questionnaire and then developed through the use of paired and group discussion, individual structured and informal discussions, observations, focus groups and reflection. A number of areas were identified for change in my personal and organisational practice. The information was recorded and discussed with participants and colleagues so that I was able '*to identify what is being looked for and plan how it can be obtained*' (Whitehead and McNiff, 2006: 63). The outcomes of the initial research identified the following:

1. The need to develop a rigorous inclusive initial assessment process from the ITT programme.

2. To provide a variety of appropriate access routes to the ITT programme to be completed within the mandatory five year period.

3. To introduce academic tutorial support.

4. To develop a process based subject specialist mentoring system.

5. To reflect, review and implement changes to assessment instruments.

The source of the continuing data for this chapter has developed through reflective practice, discussions with colleagues and more importantly working with learners on a CPD module on mentoring which involved the learners preparing and presenting seminars on a variety of aspects of mentoring, conducting small research projects and acting as mentors. I am indebted for their involvement.

Why mentoring in the FE sector

It could be argued that the FE sector now faces greater conflict and challenges to its composition and role than at any other time in its history. Whilst the Office for Educational Standards (Ofsted) found that most teacher training courses provided a good training background there was little, if any, subject specific support which would enable trainee teachers to teach in their curriculum areas. They felt that there was a lack of systematic mentoring and support in the workplace unlike teachers in the schools sector who have developed a strong culture of mentoring. The emergence of the 14-19 sector in FE compounds the need for a mentoring system and strong *'solid institutional backing'* (Cunningham 2005: 13) from government and college management with mentors efforts being recognised and rewarded. Cunningham also describes this as the *'institutional commitment to mentoring'* (p 15). This would at the very least involve recognition of the value of the mentor by allocating hours as part of their time table or/and the mentoring role being part of the criteria for promotion (Advanced Practitioner, L2 Senior Lecturer etc).

The Government Inspectorate clearly identify within ITT programmes *'…the real difficulties in 'customising' the delivery of training to meet the individual needs of an enormously diverse range of specialists'* as Cunningham points out (p 20) and the need for mentoring. Does the emphasis on the generic ITT, mentoring and focus on meeting specific subject needs offer a challenge to the prominent view? This is in contrast to a view that a subject processed-based mentoring system supports the development of *'the practical professional knowledge necessary to become competent teachers'* (Furlong and Maynard, 1995: 2). Clearly there are differing ideas about mentoring and what is necessary to support the dual professionalism of teachers in their subject area and their pedagogy.

Coaching or Mentoring

The terms mentoring and coaching appear to have become interchangeable and although given different terms arguably they both require the use of similar skills and focus on the mentees' progress. Mentoring can include aspects of teaching, counselling, instruction and information giving and requires and develops new knowledge. However, the key difference for me is about approach, attitude and development with the emphasis for mentoring being intrinsically based in Bloom's affective domain based on a person-centred approach. This is designed to develop skills, challenge attitudes and new knowledge through *'a process of change and development that goes deeper than simply gaining more knowledge'* (Wallace and Gravells, 2007: 15). In mentoring there is much potential for mutual learning. In other words *'it is not only the mentee who will benefit from the relationship'* (Wallace and Gravells, 2007: 16). This is because the mentoring process is situated learning based on refection, developing knowledge and co-continuing professional development which is a *'prime function'* of mentoring.

One of my current roles in education is to plan, prepare and deliver the Certificate and Advanced Certificate in CPD including two modules on mentoring. I outlined above that I constantly reflect and act in and on action. This includes organising focus and discussion groups with colleagues and learners to inform and enrich my reflections. An example of this from my practice is with a CPD group who were studying mentoring and initially rejected the process approach to mentoring and argued strongly for a rigid instructional coaching model that would ensure grade 1 lessons. Here the emphasis being on product outcomes to a rigid criteria and not the process of personal development. The challenge for me was to reflect on the lessons, value the learners' views and establish forms of communication that would assist me in understanding how they had come to hold their values and views. Also, to consider strategies of challenge through reflection, discussion and personal development. The views and finding for the remainder of this chapter are those of colleagues on the CPD course, members of staff from a variety of institutes and people who are on or have just completed the Cert Ed/PGCE qualification.

Whilst conducting a focus group to establish how effective the mentoring course had been all the participants commented on how much they had learnt about their personal practice from each other and their mentees. Thus endorsing the strength of a mutual process-based mentoring relationship, and demonstrating that learning *can be uniting and mutually beneficial processes* (Klasen and Clutterbuck, 2002: 18). There was also in-depth discussion about the different language that was used by those involved in a mentoring process and those who had been involved in a mentoring process based on an outcome approach. The former being seen as mentee-led and the latter led by organisational needs. The mentees reflecting on the process used words like *'guided'*, *'supported'*, *'I learnt'*, *'facilitated development'*. In contrast the mentees from the coaching-based model used words like *'informed'*, *'told'*, *'instructed'*, *'helped'*, *'told me'*, *'expertise'*, *'directed'*. It must be noted that both sets of mentees felt they had gained in a positive way from the experience, unlike their colleagues who had not received mentoring, or coaching.

The trainee mentors also reflected on the use of negotiating targets with their mentees which they felt was empowering, developed negotiation and motivational skills and identified this process as something they need to integrate into their own teaching practice. The trainees also discussed how they had developed reflective practice skills whilst modelling them and also encouraging their mentees to develop them. This would include teaching and learning strategies, specific support needs and alternatives to the negotiation and effective implementation of class rules.

Learning as a mentor: Developing a challenge to practice and personal continuing professional development as a teacher

The initial response to the question 'what is the purpose of mentoring?' to a range of trainee mentors invoked answers of *'tell and instruct the mentee on how to get a Grade 1 observation'*, clearly a rational-technical response based on a rational- technical model of teaching (Schön, 1991). The trainees accepted that this approach would be a product-led system of mentoring but genuinely believed that this would provide what the mentee needed and vigorously defended this perspective.

The challenge to the rational-technical perspective shared by the trainees was presented via a non-directive active learning task. The trainees were asked to choose and negotiate one of a range of issues to explore and reflect on and then prepare a twenty minute presentation to the group. The areas for reflection, learning and presentation selected included:

- The difference between mentoring and coaching (all the trainees felt they were the same).

- The mentoring relationship.

- The value of co-mentoring.

- The skills required for mentoring.

The outcome of the trainees' learning experience was a qualitative shift to a process- based model of mentoring, reflecting an emphasis on the value for the mentee of co-mentoring with each other and for their learners as a valuable self-directed learning experience. This value based development is a tribute to the group's high level of reflective practice.

One of the mentor trainees went on to conduct a piece of action research within catering and the uniformed services that introduced reflective practice for his learners, in an attempt to develop an understanding of constructivist learning and identifying the links between theory, functional skills, practice and understanding. Another identified in his practice, following a presentation by one of the group members on peer mentoring and co-developmental discussions, the possibility of introducing peer mentoring for groups of young mechanics who regularly present challenging behaviour. This was designed to develop skills, attitude changes, and autonomy and replace the need for disciplinary action or other behaviourist methods of management.

The implementation of a peer mentoring system was rejected at the early stages of development by his trainees with a refusal to work collectively with each other. The group member then transferred his value base and skills as a mentor and negotiated and agreed with the trainees a system of negotiated individual learning programmes which developed autonomy, and responsibility for their personal conduct and met the wishes of his trainees to learn and be responsible for their learning. This confirms that *'an individual learns through mentoring in a variety of ways'* (Klasen and Clutterbuck, 2002: 22) and also demonstrates how the learning of a mentor within the mentoring process can be transferred and implemented in a diverse range of contexts developing continuous experiential learning and professional development.

Personal refection and continuous learning

At this stage I wish to offer reflection of how and what I have leant. Reflection is a process for uncovering new knowledge and work practice. It enables the reflective practitioner to break from the rational technical models of learning to *'concrete problem solving'* (Schön, 1991: 24). Ofsted have recently highlighted the need for reflection within teaching and learning which concerns the lack of understanding of math's students. It is argued that this demonstrates the extremes of behaviourist theories that influence teaching and learning, didactical pedagogical approaches and rational technical models of teaching. Schön describes this as when, *'professional activity consist in instrumental problem solving made rigorous by the application of scientific theory and technique'* (Schön, 1991: 21) i.e. the instructional drill sergeant focused on outcome and all deficits based in the learner (the learner is the problem) as opposed to the reflective practitioner who may construct a new way of setting the problem i.e. not seeing the deficit in the learner but in the solution as within the person's practice. That is to say how I challenge, change and take ownership of my practice.

During the course of writing this chapter I have been able to challenge my developing cynicism in the teaching profession given changes in practice that are dominated by a rational technical model, by reflecting and identifying how I can still bring about change on a micro basis which enables others to challenge their practice and the dominant ideology, thus developing their learning and that of their learners. The reflective practitioner is able to challenge:

> *...the dominant technical rationality in professional education and argue for more attention to promoting artistry in teaching by reflecting 'reflection in action' and 'reflection on action' among teachers.*

(Tabachnick and Zeichner, 2005: 13)

The learners that I have been working with developed reflective practice in their teaching which subsequently informed their role within the mentoring process and in their action research. This also reinforced my learning and views on the advantages of reflective practice. My lived experience and values have shaped my personal perception of what education should be and that perception is a self-governed developmental process which enhances a feeling of worth and not simply a means to an end. Learning should be about a chosen subject matter encompassing knowledge, understanding and skill development, it should be a lifelong process at the pace that meets the learners' needs. I acknowledge that my philosophy of education falls into that advanced by Rousseau (1993) in *'Emile'* and also the *'person centred approach'* of Carl Rogers and the humanist tradition. This is the ideal.

However, I need to acknowledge the conflicting constraints of funding and government policies and priorities that through their multitude of agencies advocate the development of mentoring systems yet fail to fund them adequately. It is through the use of my critical internal and external colleagues that I am able to reflect on practice and develop a critical challenge to make change where I can.

References

Creswell. J. W. (1998) *Qualitative Inquiry and Research Design. Choosing Among Five Traditions*. London: SAGE.

Cunningham, B. (2005) *Mentoring in Post Compulsory Education a Guide to Effective Practice*. London: David Fulton Publishers.

Dreyfus, L. and Rabinow, P. (1982) *Michel Foucault Beyond Structuralism and Hermeneutics*. London: Harvester Wheatsheaf.

Foucault, M. (1982) *History of Sexuality Volume 2*. London: Penguin Books.

Furlong, J. and Maynard, T. (1995) *Mentoring Student Teachers*. London: Routledge.

Klasen, J. and Clutterbuck, D. (2002) *Implementing Mentoring Schemes: A practical Guide to Successful Programs*. Woburn MA: Butterworth-Heinmann.

McNiff, J., Lomax, P. and Whitehead. J. (2003) *You and Your Action Research Project*, (2nd edn). London: Routledge.

Ofsted (2003) *The Initial training of further education teachers*. Office for Standards in Education. London: Ofsted Publications HMI 1762.

Rogers, C. *Freedom to Learn in the 80s*. Colorado, Ohio: Merrill.

Rousseau, J. J. (1993) *Emile* (Everyman). London: Penguin Books.

Schön, D. A. (1991) *The Reflective Practitioner. How Professionals Think In Action*. London: Ashgate.

Smith, L. and Pandolfo, A. (2003) *The Construction of Difference and Bio Technico Power*. www.boltondataforinclusion.com

Tabachnick, R. and Zeichner, K. (Eds) (2005) *Issues and Practices in Inquiry Orientated Teacher Education*. London: Falmer Press.

Wallace, S. and Gravells, J. (2007) *Professional Development in the Life Long Learning Sector*. Mentoring, (2nd edn). Exeter: Learning Matters.

Whitehead, J. and McNiff, J. (2006) *Action Research Living Theory*. London: SAGE.

Teaching from a feminist agenda - the influence of feminist pedagogy on initial teacher training

Geraldine McCusker

Introduction

I have been a teacher in the further education sector for 17 years. I currently work in initial teacher training, with practitioners in the post compulsory education (PCE) sector on courses aimed at developing their professional skills and knowledge. I worked in mental health settings before I came into teaching, this move being prompted by the desire to work with people in a way that encourages their development and empowers them. My preference both then and now is to make a difference to people's lives and opportunities in my work, to support others to transcend their experiences.

In this chapter I will argue that a model of pedagogy rooted in feminist values is both essential and effective in the current PCE climate. I will argue that adopting feminist values makes for better teachers, who will then promote inclusive practice, meeting the needs of students from a range of cultural and educational backgrounds. For me engaging with feminism as a theory/philosophy helps raise awareness of imbalances, injustice and the need for making changes. Feminism also encourages reflexivity, that is, the exploration of how our values, beliefs, interests and political stances shape everything we do. Reflexivity is also essential for good teaching, a good teacher knows who s/he is and recognises that to deny the influence of one's own values in the teaching process is disingenuous for both teacher and student.

I was a feminist when I first came into teaching, and as such, practiced feminist pedagogy before I had that term in my vocabulary. In the first part of this chapter I will outline the meaning of feminism and feminist pedagogy and discuss why it is needed. The second part will share some of the practice of a feminist-informed pedagogy, presenting some ideas about how strategies based on feminist values can be incorporated into teaching. These strategies are the result of my own action research. Self-reflection is a central concept in action research, indeed, action research is a form of '*self-reflective practice*' (McNiff, 2002: online). The final part of the chapter will discuss some of the challenges feminist pedagogy brings. Here I will examine some of the tensions and share some of the unsettling experiences that often flow from the process of moving from feminist theory into feminist practice. I will suggest strategies to meet those challenges.

I hope that this chapter will act as a support to other feminist teachers as well as encourage teachers who do not identify themselves as feminists to engage with feminism as a useful theory that can help them to develop their practice. I hope that it will also help to dispel some of the myths around what is feminism and who it is for.

What is feminism?

Feminism is hard to define as it is many things to many different people; it has always been a diverse movement. In general terms one could say that it is a broad spectrum of ideas and practices that puts gender at the centre of its analysis. Gender is put at the centre so that:

• Women can demand their full rights as human beings.

• The power structures in society, the laws and conventions that keep women servile and subordinate to men, can be challenged.

• Women can work consciously together for their rights.

• The division of labour in the world that puts men in charge of the public sphere, while women work unpaid in the home taking the full responsibility for family life, can be challenged.

(Watkins *et al.*, 1992)

For me feminism is a liberating and empowering force in my life. As a young woman developing my identity, it ameliorated feelings of threat and isolation I initially experienced. I agree whole heartedly with Ann Mulvey, who when reflecting on why feminism appealed to her wrote:

> *...it affirmed my being in the world in emotional and embodied ways. It also offered tools to demystify and challenge sexist systems, and created alternative settings where I was welcomed as the person I was, not in spite of her.*

(Mulvey *et al.*, 2001: 568)

Feminism is central to my work. It is at the core of my professional practice and as a teacher and researcher I am motivated to advance feminist knowledge, action and debate. After Fine (1992: vii), I see myself as an activist and aim to:

> *...press, provoke, and unbalance social inequities that choreograph relations of gender, race, class, disability and sexuality.*

I want to contribute to knowledge and understanding about how to support social justice and human liberation. For me feminism is a means to make things better not just for myself but for others too.

What is feminist pedagogy?

Feminist pedagogy is closely aligned to other critical pedagogies such as those espoused by Freire (1973) and Giroux (1988), both of whom acknowledged how important it is for teachers to recognise power relations in the classroom.

In discussing critical pedagogy, Clarke (2002: 67) suggested:

> *Teachers engaged in critical pedagogy are united in a view of education as a practice committed to the reduction, or even elimination, of injustice and oppression.*

As well as being emancipatory, feminist pedagogy also (and importantly) interrogates gender relations, recognising that sexism is a pervasive ideology and that learning environments are gendered. Feminist teachers and educators not only want to empower students, but also want to examine the role gender plays in that empowerment process. It also takes account of complex identities and multiple sites of oppression or inequality:

> *Feminist and liberatory pedagogies aim to encourage the students - particularly white women, working class students, and members of under-represented ethnic groups - to gain an education that would be relevant to their concerns, to create their own meanings, and to find their own voices in relation to the material.*

> (Maher and Thompson-Tetreault, 2001: 3)

Traditional pedagogical styles can make women passive and invisible (Maher, 1985), whilst in contrast feminist pedagogy is an enabling, inspiring and motivating pedagogy, that fosters resistance and encourages critical thinking (hooks, 1989; Lather, 1991; Morley, 1999; Mauthner, 2009). Importantly it makes a strong link between the individual and society which is particularly relevant to education:

Feminist pedagogy reflects the women's movement's juxtaposition of the personal with the political. As such, changes start in the micro politics of the classroom.

> (Morley, 1998: 16)

Why a feminist pedagogy is crucial

Gender inequalities still exist even though many achievements have been made. This is both nationally as well as globally:

> *The vast majority of the world's women still have very little power, at work, in their relationships at home, or in the wider social world.*

> (Van der Gaag, 2004: 10)

It is important to remember that students in the PCE sector are diverse in terms of their ethnic background and many will originate from countries where women's rights are not on the agenda. A teacher adopting a feminist pedagogy can empower such students or expose some of the issues which otherwise may remain invisible.

Although women gained the vote in the UK, have equal pay and antidiscrimination legislation and have achieved much, women's rights have still not been fully attained. There is still therefore much work to do and indeed women are in danger of losing some of the rights that have been won (Van der Gaag, 2004). Recently Kira Cochrane sounded an alarm call when she detailed what she views as an all out assault on feminism and identified:

> *The sex industry is booming, the rape conviction rate is plummeting, women's bodies are picked over in the media, abortion rights are under serous threat and top business leaders say they don't want to employ women.*

(Cochrane, 2008: 6)

Women are still not represented fully in positions of power. Only 19.3% of members of parliament are women, women are still underrepresented in science, the judiciary and in business (Cooke, 2008).

Campaigning in a similar vein, Jessica Ringrose advocated the teaching of feminism in schools, arguing that there is an absence of strong female role models for girls and one consequence is that many are struggling to find a positive identity and often their identity is defined by their sexuality (TES, 2008).

This is something that resonates strongly with my experiences. I recently observed a class of ten female 17 year olds in a lesson based around the general topic of self esteem. The tutor I was observing was asked to come in to deliver the session because there had been instances of bullying amongst the group. What I witnessed was a group of young women disempowered by their gender and their social class. Some telling incidents for me were when as an introductory exercise the tutor asked if all could introduce themselves using an adjective that begins with the same letter as their first name. In response to the example of Fearsome Fiona sadly, '*Sexy Samantha*', '*Randy Rebecca*', and '*Saucy Sue*' were amongst the initial suggestions offered. A later activity asked them to identify what factors have positive and negative effects on their self esteem. These were then categorised as external (outside of themselves and beyond their control) or internal (from themselves and so within their control). They were unable to offer any internal suggestions and so all suggestions were external and included boyfriends, getting compliments, getting spots and getting a pay rise.

On this occasion I also considered that the language of the tutor contributed to the sense of disempowerment I recognised in the room. One aspect of the tutor's behaviour that I urged her to reflect on as a priority, both in terms of her professional identity as a teacher and as not reproducing sexist values in the classroom, was the use of the word 'Guys' when addressing the students. 'Guys' originated as a gendered term. This term is now used extensively in the popular media aimed at young people, as a collective term for females and males. It is important that as teachers working with young people we should not adopt this term uncritically and where possible we should open up a discussion about it. This would be better than simply adopting it as language that is used that reflects the dominant perspective and male as standard. When male terms are used to embrace both female and male they have the effect of muting the female, this then becomes self perpetuating (Spender, 1985).

Another pressing reason for a feminist pedagogy is the current concern about levels of sexual violence. Womankind Worldwide, a charity working with schools and local authorities to develop resources to counter sexual bullying and raise awareness of violence against women, produced a report in which they identified that there is still an alarming prevalence of attitudes that reinforce violent behaviours towards women. A recommendation from the study was that teacher training needs to stress gender inequality as a core part of teachers' theoretical and practical framework. If this engagement with gender equality debates is achieved then teachers should feel as confident and skilled in facilitating debate that challenges gender inequality as they do in delivering their subject (Womankind Worldwide, 2007).

The need to make the classroom a place where gender inequalities can be openly discussed was also echoed by Jessica Ringrose (Paton, 2008: online) who points out that:

> *We need to find a place in the curriculum to look at violence against women and sexist bullying. Girls may do better than boys in tests, but it doesn't matter how they perform academically, they still don't get paid as much in the work place.*

Bell (2008) posed the question of why derogatory terms for females are not given the same gravitas as racist or homophobic bullying. Her article on the growing problem of sexual bullying in schools makes uncomfortable reading as she identifies how popular culture encourages a particular view of women and reinforces the message that it is acceptable to bully females and behave in a violent way towards them. Sexual humiliation is almost a national sport in some areas of popular media. This is the backdrop for teachers. Embracing a feminist pedagogy would help teachers counter some of this and help them to empower their students to challenge some of the more negative aspects of current popular trends. Bloom (2009) reported the concerns of Neil Duncan, of Wolverhampton University who has identified an urgent need to address sexual bullying in British schools.

This is an international and global issue, and writers in the U.S. have also recognised that a feminist pedagogy is vital to critically engage with social injustice, bullying and discrimination. Laura Larson writes:

> *...feminist pedagogy is an essential tool both to deconstruct and to make meaning of the current manifestations of inequality in U.S. society. It provides educators with the means to help students integrate emotional responses to social injustices with cognitive learning. Given the current climate, feminist pedagogy is essential to promoting critical thinking and reflection that leads to transformative learning, student empowerment and collective action.*

> (Larson, 2005: 135)

How can you apply principles of feminist pedagogy in practice?

Praxis (putting theory into action) is a core idea of feminism, so in this section I will offer strategies based on key feminist principles of empowerment, reflexivity, participation and collaboration, which can be used to inform teaching practice. I will examine different stages of the teaching process and recommend strategies that would support the development of a feminist pedagogy.

The strategies recommended are based on my own critical reflections. Critical reflection is itself an emancipatory process and a means by which we can have a more developed view about our practice (Hillier, 2005). The strategies represent findings from my adoption of the methodological principles of action research based upon a cycle of action and reflection. I present them as examples of insider knowledge, and they can be used in other settings. They should be interpreted as action research as they are evidence that comes from engagement with actions that placed at their heart the value of social justice for all, and they provide knowledge and understanding of how political and social contexts shape human activity (Somekh, 2006).

Planning

All good teachers recognise the important role planning plays in ensuring an effective session. As a teacher working from a feminist perspective it is helpful to use the planning stage to carefully consider the needs of a teaching group in terms of gender, race, disability and social class and actively promote non–sexist, anti racist and anti-oppressive strategies at every opportunity. For example if time is not planned in for nominated questions and equal chances for student contributions, it is likely that some students might dominate discussions while others go unheard.

It is also possible to empower students by involving them in the planning. One could negotiate how the course could be run, for example. Or, simply have a policy where negotiation is a possibility to be integrated where and when appropriate. This will also promote participation and collaborative learning and help students to realise the benefit of both.

Resources

When deciding on the resources to use, a feminist teacher should make a conscious effort to use positive and non-stereotypical role models where applicable. It is important to model this in practice, as exposure to non-stereotypical role models is an important step in reducing prejudice.

Games and puzzles used in teaching should reflect the cultural and social experiences of students. For example, it is important not to assume that every one understands and is interested in football. It is still a male dominated sport. If used it needs to be acknowledged that it is a male dominated sport.

Another strategy is to consciously use examples of work by females. If every researcher, theorist, artist or writer referred to is male it marginalises the achievements of women and can give the message that male achievement is greater than female achievement. It is also important to have an awareness of the portrayal of women, men, ethnic minorities and those defined as having a disability in resources, as well as raising this awareness in your students. When using materials that come from a member of a privileged group ensure students are aware that the privilege will have impacted on that person's ability to be a leading light in their field.

Delivery - teaching and managing learning

The delivery of lessons is influenced by a variety of factors, but key to delivery is how the teacher presents themselves. It is important to be conscious of the use of language and avoid language that has sexist connotations. Using 'he', 'his', 'man' and 'mankind' as generic terms is not acceptable as these are not inclusive terms. The incongruence of using 'man' as a generic term was highlighted to me recently. I observed a teacher teaching in a women's prison and read a report from a previous observer who had commented: '*The atmosphere was friendly yet workmanlike*'. In this context the use of '*workma*n' stood out as a very awkward and inappropriate term.

Jokes that rely on sexual innuendo should be avoided. Inappropriate sexual references as well as causing embarrassment can often be very offensive. Sexism is often the basis of such jokes. Every opportunity should be taken to look at language in a very explicit way with students, especially when teaching a language. Encourage critical skills in students by getting them to respond to language and concepts by putting them in their social, political and cultural context. Remember that language is never neutral (Spender, 1985).

If sexism, racism or other forms of prejudice occur then this should be challenged rather than ignored. It is good practice to discuss issues as they arise. When looking at scientific subjects discuss the unscientific bias of claims used to justify sexism and show how far from being objective such theories are value laden and influenced by past social and political interests. Emphasise the subjective nature of history and historical data. It is still *his* story. Women's experiences are often marginalised or hidden/ignored.

Relationships in the classroom

Collaboration should be encouraged by creating an atmosphere of support and shared goals in the classroom. Facilitate discussions around students' concerns, fears and hopes, from this they could then help each other, reducing feelings of isolation that students sometimes experience. It has long been recognised that equal status contact helps to reduce prejudice, encouraging personal contact on an equal basis between members of different groups in classes will be helping to counter the development of prejudice (Cook and Pelfrey, 1985).

Supporting students

It is important to be sensitive to and supportive of the outside responsibilities that students have. Often female students have family responsibilities that are very demanding. These may conflict with their studies and a flexible approach may be needed to respond to this. Violence and learning for example is a problem that has recently been highlighted. Appleby (2008) identifies that often the people we teach, especially in the lifelong learning sector, are dealing with hidden issues including violence as a significant aspect of their life experiences. She advocates that we can support such students by raising our own awareness of violence and in particular gendered violence. A good starting point for this is the violence and learning website (www.learningandviolence.net). This site was launched in Canada in 2006, as an interactive educational tool to help change the face of education, so that in situations where learning takes place in a context of violence, education can be more effective. One of its goals is to build a better, deeper understanding of the issue of violence and learning.

Reflection on practice

Reflecting honestly should be a regular part of practice. Incorporate challenging questions such as: 'Have I included all students today?' 'Have I used inclusive language?' 'Could any of my behaviour be viewed as marginalising any of the students?' 'Have I responded to the needs of my students in a fair and transparent way?' Many of these things are of course difficult to achieve on a daily basis but we need to continually reflect on this part of practice especially as teachers are increasingly being driven by external productivity measures.

What are the challenges of applying feminist values?

It has to be said that identifying oneself as a feminist in a classroom is often met with mixed responses. Sometimes these responses are negative. Some students see it as a barrier and work hard to undermine or find fault as a means of disempowering. This can also sometimes manifest itself in aggressive or confrontational language and behaviour. It can also mean being accused of being a biased teacher, who gives too much emphasis to gender. This is particularly true when delivering a session around gender equality, as I often find I am. I counter this by ensuring that in this instance the session is meticulously planned and all my arguments are supported by well researched evidence from a variety of credible sources.

Others may view feminism as a barrier because for them feminism is a slogan for idealists, for those who want more than equality or for those who are living in some kind of a time warp. In such circumstances it can be seen as an opportunity to introduce a new element into the classroom - getting a reaction by being antifeminist. This challenge to a teacher's authority can be difficult to manage because going along with the jokes is condoning antifeminism, while not doing so will be seen as reinforcing the stereotype that feminists are humourless. Student resistance to feminism can often take the form of challenging the authority of the feminist teacher (Lawthom and Burman, 1999).

Another possible tension in introducing feminism in the classroom is that some students can feel disempowered and uncertain if traditional boundaries are seen to be blurred. When these students are women or from other marginalised groups this can be doubly hurtful. In this scenario it really feels like doing a disservice to your students and feminist ideals. Another possible reaction is that feminism can be good for students but not so good for the teacher. Sometimes students can identify with the teacher too much and there can be an expectation that s/he should respond in a supportive and flexible manner to every demand made. Sometimes there is the expectation for someone with feminist principles to take on more than a fair share of the responsibility for the relational aspects of the work in a team:

> *Feminist teachers often struggle to maintain a delicate balance in pedagogy between over/under feeding students. A challenge is how to facilitate student development, without assuming the role of surrogate mother.*
>
> (Shaw, 1995: 146)

An important question arising from this discussion of how the feminist teacher is challenged, is the issue of why people feel so threatened by feminism. The answer lies in the fact that it is a critical perspective that challenges long held assumptions. A negative reaction is a common response to novel ideas and so this makes it important to tread carefully, particularly when students may experience a sense of losing something by challenging the status quo. Students, often reforming their own identities, may find change both liberating and at the same time disconcerting. This may sometimes lead to students wanting to hold onto a perceived or actual privileged position that provides some measure of personal power:

> *The resistance to the spread of feminist principles and methodologies by those who are privileged by the prevailing social order has been sustained and widespread.*
>
> (Dominelli, 2002: 104)

Is it possible to respond to these challenges?

One obvious response is to look for the positives that come from feminism. I have been fortunate to have witnessed the burgeoning feminism in many of my students. I am passing the message on. Many women students have thanked me for helping them find solutions to the sexism they have been subjected to in their lives. They feel they have been liberated and are now more in control of their lives. As one student said to me '*I don't blame myself or my mother anymore, I am free of that guilt and hostility*'.

Another positive outcome from practising feminist pedagogy came in an interaction I had with a beauty therapy teacher who, aware of my recognition of language as a tool for oppression was concerned not to use 'Ladies' in my presence when I was observing her class, and came up with 'Therapists' instead. During her lesson she addressed her young women students as therapists on a number of occasions, when in the past she would have used 'Ladies'. Reflecting on this experience she concluded that it felt so much better to call them therapists as it was a more professional and dignifying term, which of course it is, because, unlike 'Ladies' it does not buy into value judgements and act as a negative constraint on behaviour.

Finding like-minded colleagues with whom to share experiences in a supportive relationship is another good way to respond. This chapter is itself a way to respond to the challenges. In the spirit of feminist thinking I am not confining my experiences to the domain of private discussion, but am telling my stories here to a wider audience.

Reflections

The writing of this chapter has been a fulfilling and empowering experience for me. It has reaffirmed my belief in the practice of feminist pedagogy. I began this chapter in the winter of 2008 under the shadow of a restructure in my college, a restructure that would result in the loss of my manager, another practitioner of feminist pedagogy with whom I have enjoyed a supportive relationship. As the chapter is being finalised she has now left and so working on finalising this chapter has been an important cathartic process to help me through the current transition.

The opportunity to reflect on my own pedagogical processes has been very important to me. I have also enjoyed many of the collaborative aspects of this project. Some colleagues have been supportive and taken the opportunity to share with me their own experiences of sexism and have said they feel that such a discussion is vitally needed.

However, while I am in reflective mood it is worth saying that my declaration that my chapter would look at feminist pedagogy has received a mixed response. In discussions with my colleagues I have picked up a range of reactions, some of the more negative reactions have included silence, apathy and disengagement with the discussion. I was not unprepared for this, as I know the feminist perspective is so far removed from mainstream views on pedagogy that any vigorous promotion of it will be likely to evoke such reactions, as the acclaimed cultural critic bell hooks has astutely observed:

> *Feminist pedagogy can only be liberatory if it is truly revolutionary because the mechanisms of approbation within white supremacist, capitalist patriarchy are able to co-opt with tremendous ease that which merely appears radical or subversive.*

(hooks, 1989: 50-51)

References

Appleby, Y. (2008) Literacy matters, violence, literacy and learning, *Research and Practice in Adult Literacy*, No 65, 47-54.

Bell, R. (2008) *That joke isn't funny anymore*. The Guardian. 4 November 2008 p3.

Bloom, A. (2009) *Sexual bullying 'has always gone on'*. Times Educational Supplement. [website] Available from <www.tes.co.uk > [Retrieved 20 March 2009].

Clarke, J. (2002) Deconstructing domestication: women's experience and the goals of critical pedagogy, in: R. Harrison, F. Reeve, A. Hanson and J. Clarke (Eds), *Supporting lifelong learning Volume 1: perspectives on learning*, 62-77. London: Routledge /Falmer and Open University.

Cochrane, K. (2008) *Now, the backlash*. The Guardian, 1st July 2008 pg 6-11.

Cook, S. W. and Pelfrey, M. (1985) Reactions to being helped in cooperating inter-racial groups. *Journal of Personality and Social Psychology* 49,1231-45.

Cooke, R. (2008) *How far have we come in 80 years? Post –feminist backlash- or new dawn for equal rights?* The Observer, 7 December 2008.

Dominelli, L. (2002) Feminist Theory, in: M. Davies (Ed.) *The Blackwell Companion to Social Work,* (p96 -106). Oxford: Blackwell publishing.

Fine, M. (1992) *Disruptive Voices. The Possibilities of Feminist Research*. Michigan: The University of Michigan Press.

Freire, P. (1973) *Pedagogy of the Oppressed*. Harmonsworth: Penguin.

Giroux, H. (1988) *Schooling and the Struggle for Public Life: Critical Pedagogy in the Modern Age*. Minneapolis. MN: University of Minnesota Press.

Hillier, Y. (2005) *Reflective Teaching in Further and Adult Education*, (2nd edn). Continuum.

hooks, b. (1989) *Talking Back: Thinking Feminist, Thinking Black*. London: Sheba.

Larson, L. M. (2005) The Necessity of Feminist Pedagogy in a Climate of Political Backlash. *Equity and Excellence in Education*, vol 38 issue 2 May 2005 135-144.

Lather, P. (1991) *Getting Smart: Feminist Research and Pedagogy with/in the Post modern*. London: Routledge.

Lawthom, R. and Burman, E. (1999) Tensions and possibilities of feminist authority in post-compulsory education. *Educational and Child Psychology*, vol.16 (2) 151-164.

Maher, F. (1985) Classroom pedagogy and the new scholarship on women, in: M.Culley and C. Portuges (Eds), *Gendered Subjects: The Dynamics of Feminist Teaching*. London and New York: Routledge and Kegan Paul p 29-48.

Maher, F. A. and Thompson Tetreault, M.K (2001) *The Feminist Classroom Dynamics of Gender, Race and Privilege*. Maryland: Rowman and Littlefield Publishers Inc.

Mauthner, M. (2009) Feminist Pedagogy [website] Available from <www.ioe.ac.uk/learningmatters/peddebate.hjm> [Retrieved 14 January 2009].

Mc Niff, J. (2002) *Action research for professional development. Concise advice for new action researchers* [website] Available from <www.jeanmcniff.com/booklet/html> [Retrieved 19 September 2008].

Morley, L. (1998) All you need is love: feminist pedagogy for empowerment and emotional labour in the academy. *International Journal of Inclusive Education* vol 2, No 1 15-2y.

Morley, L. (1999) *Organising Feminisms: the Micro politics of the Academy*. Basingstoke: Macmillan.

Mulvey, A., Gridley, H., Gawith, L. (2001) Convent Girls, Feminism, and Community Psychology, *Journal of Community Psychology* vol 29, No 5, 563-584.

Paton, G. (2008) *'Schools should teach feminism in the classroom'* The Telegraph [website] Available from <www.telegraph.co.uk/education> [Retrieved 14 January 2009].

Shaw, J. (1995) *Education, Gender and Anxiety*. London: Taylor and Francis.

Somekh, B. (2006) *Action Research a methodology for change and development*. Maidenhead: Open University Press.

Spender, D. (1985) *Man Made Language*, (2nd edn). London and New York: Routledge and Kegan Paul.

TES, (2008) Schools urged to teach feminism *Times Educational Supplement* [website] Available from <www.tes.co.uk > [Retrieved 14 January 2009].

Van der Gaag, N. (2004) What women have gained in the fight for equality with men - and what they are in danger of losing. *New Internationalist* Nov 2004 pg 9-12.

Watkins, S. A., Rueda, M., Rodriquez, M. (1992) *Feminism for Beginners*. Cambridge: Icon books Ltd.

Womankind Worldwide, (2007) Challenging Violence Changing Lives Gender on the *UK Education Agenda Findings and Recommendations 2004 -2007* [website] Available from <www.womankind.org.uk> [Retrieved 22 November 2007].

Supporting initial teacher trainees with learning differences

Paul Smith

At the time of writing I have taught in the further education (FE) sector for twenty five years and for the last eight years have delivered initial teacher training (ITT) programmes for FE teachers that is validated by a university. During this time education and training has been transformed. Beset by a myriad of changes in policy and expectations, the FE sector's identity has become lost in the flurry of new initiatives where even its name has lost continuity. These changes have led to new pressures for those working in a sector that is controlled by an inverted pyramid of non-governmental organisations. The very character of the FE sector has changed rapidly with academic subjects such as Advanced Subsidiary (AS) and A Level (A2) increasingly the domain of school sixth forms and the FE colleges moving further towards a predominantly vocational model. The staffing profile has also changed with increased casualisation of staffing, marginalisation of experienced lecturers and a genuine concern that professionalism is being subverted by top-down professionalisation (Cunningham, 2005; Shain, 1998).

In recent years it has become more apparent, in my own practice as a teacher trainer that as the staffing profile changes, many teacher trainees lack the skills or experience in working at a higher education level with some carrying significant negative learning experiences with them. In most cases these trainees are able to adapt to the required level and to progress successfully towards their qualification. However, up to ten per cent of trainees on the Certificate /Post Graduate Certificate in Education programmes that I deliver have a learning difference, specific or non-specific traits, and usually undiagnosed, which impacts upon their ability to complete assignments. Such trainees may display dyslexic tendencies, language processing issues, audio processing challenges or autistic spectrum characteristics. In my experience, these trainees are not spread evenly across the curriculum with greater numbers of learning differences evident when the trainees teach Art and Design, Hair and Beauty, Outdoor Education, Information and Learning Technology and Construction although, here too one needs to be careful not to label such trainees since the issue is not confined to these subjects.

The question teacher training providers need to address therefore, is how can we help those displaying learning differences to successfully attain their initial teaching qualification and make progress in their own learning and development? The position adopted in this chapter is that it may be the assessment strategies used in ITT programmes that is creating the difficulties faced by teacher trainees, that ITT is disabling some new entrants to the profession by using assessments focused upon the written word when other forms of assessment could be used allowing these trainees to use the skills they do possess. However, before the issue of assessment is addressed one needs to consider some broader issues.

Factors influencing the provision of learning support

Funding changes mean that it is harder to put appropriate support for teacher trainees with specific learning difficulties (SpLD) or non-specific learning difficulties into place. It is now a requirement that such support has to be costed and funds accessed before the support is given to the trainee. This in turn requires an assessment of SpLD followed by an application for funding through the Disabled Student's Allowance (DSA) and the assessment of need by the higher education institution (HEI). Fees charged by HEIs also vary between institutions. In the context of a two year part time route, time is available for initial assessments to be made and strategies put into place but only if the learning difference is identified at interview/recruitment or in the early stages such as by way of diagnostic and initial assessments. Even when we have made checks at these stages an underlying characteristic may remain hidden because the trainee may not wish to disclose their difficulties or have already developed coping strategies of their own and want to continue using these. Teacher trainees rarely volunteer how long it has taken them to do a piece of homework when they are struggling and therefore it can be difficult for teacher trainers to identify a learning support issue. For trainees completing their ITT qualification in one year, the issue of early identification and implementation of support is even more critical.

The study support teams I have worked with offer excellent levels of support to teacher trainees usually in the form of initial screening leading onto individual tutorials to identify strategies for learners to manage their challenges either on a generic basis or with respect to particular assignments. Many resources and strategies are available including software options that can be used by some trainees and decisions are made as to which are the most useful for their development. Once a learning issue has been identified trainees are usually offered one to one support with a study support specialist and this allows for focused, individually tailored support to be implemented. Such support has been particularly successful in helping teacher trainees develop their writing styles and has been very well received by the trainees many of whom had not considered that they had a characteristic for which support was available prior to joining the initial teacher training programmes.

Accessing funding for this support, however, is complex with restrictions in place such as funding being related to teacher trainee's prior acquisition of a student loan. HEIs fund according to percentage need and institution-specific needs. It is common in my own experience for FE colleges to pay for a trainee's DSA statement because the funds are not forthcoming from a partner HEI. Even with a DSA statement of need the entitlement is for a recommended maximum of ten tutorials. If any more support tutorials are needed the tutor/trainee have to re-apply for funding but given delays in processing the new application, this decision needs to be made after the fifth or sixth tutorial to maintain continuity of support. Inherent in this is a misunderstanding about the impact of learning differences on the completion of assignments during a one or two year course. It is assumed that ten sessions will be enough to resolve the learning issue. However, language processing differences, for example, are often long term and re-appear throughout the study period. Progress in managing learning differences is characterised by stop-start, forward-reverse dynamics and confusion over problem solving strategies resulting in variable rates of progress. It is difficult for colleagues providing study support to meet the teacher trainee's needs in such a restricted allocation of time.

A further issue arises when we consider the option of providing in-class assistants for teacher trainees with language processing differences. It is the convention to use in-class assistants with 16-19 year old learners as they study for their qualifications but the matter adopts a different proportion when we consider teacher trainees. Inclusivity requires us to treat all learners equally and for learners with a physical difference for example deafness, blindness or motor difficulties, it is common practice to use in-class assistants and other resources, for which funding is available. Yet, where the support issue focuses upon literacy, an issue often hidden to the trainee's colleagues, there is a different and specific need for sensitivity. There is a burden of expectation, although this remains a matter of debate, that teachers should be able to demonstrate appropriate levels of literacy in the performance of their teaching role. However, to identify a class member to be in need of an in-class assistant, challenges the individual's sense of identity and can be an invasion of the person's right to choose, have self-esteem consequences and impact upon their status in the group. Therefore, the motivation to provide learning support may well be informed by inclusive practice but the outcome may be to exclude and yet equally, the decision not to provide such support may also be anti-inclusive. The use of in-class assistants on teacher training programmes is a decision that we may need to make but this has to be done with a great deal of sensitivity to the learner involved and be based upon an informed decision conforming to the trainee's own choices.

In approaching the issue of teachers with learning differences it is important to avoid constructing a discourse that defines the need for learning support as a problem either for the learner or the training provider. The danger in adopting deficit models is that blame or agency lies with the trainee's inability to adapt to an established requirement. It is clear that the outcome of initial teacher training programmes is that the trainees must be appropriately qualified to work as a teacher in the sector and this standard has to be maintained. However, to problematise the issue can lead all concerned into the untenable position where individuals with learning differences are not allowed to teach. In the present circumstances, if this position was to be adopted, there would be a large number of teachers in FE whose posts would be called into question.

The conventional response, particularly under the 2002 Disability Discrimination Act, is to argue that appropriately focused support should be offered to the trainee and it is their responsibility to take advantage of the development opportunity. In this way 'reasonable adjustments' can be made by the institution and conformity to the DDA established. However, where funding for the assessment process is not available, institutions can only offer limited support which does not actually meet the needs of the trainee but allows the institution to claim compliance to the DDA. This can further be seen as a way to locate the cause of the learning difference with the teacher trainee rather than the provision of learning.

Providing learning support

In recent years I have worked with teacher trainees who have experienced literacy based learning differences and this has impacted upon their ability to produce written assignments to the required standard. These trainees had the proverbial 'spiky profile' where they often possessed excellent subject specific skills, very good verbal communication skills, above average intelligence and were highly motivated to succeed. Their needs became apparent in initial screening tasks at interview, during diagnostic assessments, or during the initial contacts and exchanges in the classroom. It was clear in all situations that it was inappropriate to let the trainees repeat submissions of their assignments because they were essentially encountering the same literacy obstacles and repetition and re-writing was not going to help them achieve. At such stages it is incumbent upon teacher trainers to reflect on their approach. Schön (1983) refers to this as *'reflection in action'* and makes a pertinent distinction between this form of thinking and *'reflection on action'*.

One teacher trainee I worked with was an excellent teacher with huge motivation levels, was very conscientious, articulate in class and developed very creative approaches to teaching and learning. However, it became apparent when she started missing deadlines and in subsequent tutorials that she was spending too long completing assignments and when she was asked to submit early copies of her work it was clear that she was exhibiting language processing issues with her written work characterised by repetition, a confusion in explanations of terms and concepts, a lack of pattern and direction and an inability to expand the debate to incorporate additional ideas.

After discussions with a colleague in study support, tutorials were arranged to consider strategies for writing assignments but the issues persisted and were reinforced by an anxiety over failing the course. Having tried support with writing strategies we adopted a *viva voce* model for an assignment. This required a different form of expression at which the learner excelled. Time spent on preparation was reduced and the outcome was a success for the trainee. It was clear to me from this experience that had we identified the issue earlier we would have been able to respond more effectively to the learner need. More specifically, that it was the assessment process that the trainee was not coping with and not the understanding of principles.

A second teacher trainee offered a different challenge. This person had difficulties grasping new information in class whilst her written work tended to be thin on content and analysis, descriptive and with the discussion prone to misinterpretations. During initial assessments with the study support team this trainee found it difficult to complete timed activities and copying speed was slow but she also showed very good spelling capabilities and a very strong coping strategy based upon a visual-spatial imagination of concepts and ideas. In short, her test results revealed that although she experienced difficulties these would not be enough to trigger support through a DSA assessment but that they would impinge upon her ability to express her learning. She was very quick to pick up on ideas and even took the strategies identified into her own teaching to help her learners. Here too her assignment work improved although study support continued to be accessed for subsequent assignments but as no DSA was available, this was at a cost to the college.

The issue here is not that these and other teacher trainees progressed but that the programme based assessment format almost caused them to fail and that this was the trigger for their difficult experience, not their ability to teach nor their understanding of teaching and learning principles. This immediately forces us to consider how we are assessing learning on initial teacher training programmes. With the exception of the observation of teaching practice and in-class presentations, it is the norm for the majority of formal assessment to be based on written assignments. As a result trainees who we know to have difficulties with this form of assessment are actually being disadvantaged. The very programme that relates theories of learning styles and differentiation to these trainees is the same programme that is creating barriers to the successful completion of their professional qualification. The clear outcome for those who deliver initial teacher training programmes is therefore that we have to re-consider how we assess learning, with the particular view that we need to open up assessment patterns to reflect the ability of the trainees and not the ease by which we can monitor their ability. This does not mean that we should change the topics of assessment but more creative ways to record the assessments are required. Nor does it mean that teacher trainees able to cope with the written assignments should be forced to complete alternative strategies. What it does mean is that there is a need for flexible interpretation of assignments combined with the scope for differential evidencing of knowledge, skills and understanding.

Viva voce has been used in universities for many years to assess understanding. The strength of this 'living voice' lies in the opportunity to informally discuss issues pertinent to the assignment content. Questions can be constructed to meet the demands of the learning outcomes, the advice of learning support specialists and the skills base of the trainee. For trainees who may spend hours repeating written assignments struggling with the transfer of concepts and ideas in their heads onto paper, this is clearly a way forward. Often written assignments are submitted with the same points repeated throughout the piece and with limited development of other points. The questioning process will provide the structure and focus the trainee's attention on a range of points to be considered thereby giving them the opportunity to demonstrate their knowledge, skills and understanding. Here the trainee's study time can be focussed upon the subject content rather than any difficulties with language processing for text. The skills of the questioner can be used to ensure that all the learning outcomes are achieved whilst the evidence for the achievement lies in the recording of the trainee's responses. This in turn can be made available to moderators or external examiners to ensure compatibility with standards.

Video can be used to record presentations, participation in activities or discussions and as an alternative to direct observation and in these ways can evidence a trainee's teaching ability. It can also be used to support ILT based evidence such as a PowerPoint or other form of presentations using computing technology as a medium. Construction of learning resources such as interactive games should be used as evidence not only of ILT knowledge and skills but also of subject content. The Jisc initiative (www.info@jisc.ac.uk) and the National Learning Network (www.help@nln.ac.uk) amongst others have sought to promote the expansion of e-learning and both show how video and e-learning lends itself very well to the assessment process on an initial teacher training programme.

Mind maps are an excellent way to represent knowledge and understanding and are appropriate for many learners with language processing difficulties. They are flexible, encourage multi-lateral thinking and can show linkages between concepts or ideas. With the increasingly available use of mind map software such as Inspiration (www.techready.co.uk/inspiration) or the Tony Buzan based imindmap (www.buzanonline.com) the expression of a teacher trainee's understanding can become a complex statement where previously hesitant or understated expressions of understanding were evident. Mind maps offer a framework for some learners through which they can express their knowledge and understanding and can be used in planning learning, delivery and assessment. As such they make an ideal and flexible tool for trainees and a realistic alternative to written assessments.

Group work can be harnessed in assessment. It offers an excellent teaching and learning methodology combined with a strong assessment opportunity. Differentiation is built into the format, group dynamics are clearly evidenced and grading, if required, can be derived from the overall product with each member sharing a mark either as a whole group or weighted by group members according to their individual contributions. Witness statements commonly used across the vocational curriculum can be used to record attainment where a competence model is preferred and no grading is required. Portfolios of achievement could be used to record contributions to group work and be made available for moderation.

Investigative projects based upon collaborative learning when used successfully provide a very productive learning experience and can be applied to any aspect of an initial teacher training programme. This can be by way of classroom based activities or through strategies such as peer observations. The collaborative element has long term benefits not only for the training period but when used successfully can become the basis of developing an ethos of sharing experiences which can also lead onto the creation of a collaborative culture throughout an FE college (Peterson, 1994). This is an example of where initial teacher training can establish a core principle that can be embedded into learner's personal practice which, in turn can inform the debate in FE colleges to the betterment of institutions and working relationships.

The quality that each of these strategies possess is that the assessment lies in the doing of an activity rather than writing about it. There will still be a requirement to record evidence on paper for portfolios, or ILT based alternatives, but the evidence can be on proforma rather than in traditional essay or report formats. It is the latter two that generate the difficulties for the teacher trainees with learning differences or those from non-academic backgrounds and so, as a matter of inclusion, ITT providers need to consider how the assessment patterns they use can be modified to allow the full recognition of a teacher's knowledge and skills base.

Implications for ITT providers

Under the DDA inclusivity is a right not a privilege and therefore the barriers that are generated by traditional assessment patterns with roots in the university sector's emphasis upon written assignments, need to be removed. The majority of initial teacher trainees in FE colleges possess a Level Three qualification on entry to their programme. For the majority of these their employer does not request higher level qualifications because in many instances the occupational competencies are more prized and readily available than a Level Four qualification. This may be changing with the advancement of foundation degrees and the requirement for higher level qualifications but at the moment there are not enough potential entrants to the sector with Level Four qualifications in place. ITT providers need to accept trainees' ability levels and to focus upon assessing the knowledge and skills these trainees are able to demonstrate, rather than those that are possessed by the minority of trainees from academic backgrounds.

ITT providers also need to look closely at their portfolio of courses. Multiple routes through to qualification are now required which means that teacher trainees should be given different options, according to their ability and experience, that will maximise their chances of success. Combining Level Three certification with appropriate study skills packages and other professional awards with the option of developing teaching experience prior to moving onto a Level Four qualification, is a more productive strategy than trying to force all trainees through a Level Four qualification from the start. At present the requirement is that trainees complete their Level Four qualification within five years of starting. Using this qualification period can only benefit the trainees. Of course the learning differences discussed in this chapter will not disappear with a longer study period but the trainees will have more opportunity to progress if they are given more time to devise coping strategies and the emphasis on written assessment is diminished.

ITT providers will also need to look at their initial and diagnostic strategies. In recent years we have used two pieces of handwritten work at the interview stage as a means of identifying trainees who may have characteristics that will require support whilst they are on the course. It is explained to all interviewees that this is a screening exercise and not a barrier to entry. This has been effective in signalling support issues but we are also conscious that this needs some refinement and initial on course assignments, and further screenings are closely monitored for learning differences. The early identification of any learning support issues is equally as imperative as redesigning the on course assessment strategy.

The core theme of the argument presented here is that ITT providers must ensure that they give due recognition to everyone's right of access to progression opportunities and signal an end to discriminatory practice. We need to celebrate the diversity of those learners beginning their initial teacher training and adapt our practice to their needs. The argument certainly offers a challenge to academic conventions and the existing models of assessment. It also highlights the paradox inherent in the professionalization of the workforce where we are employing more teachers from a non-HE background but expecting them to gain recognised HE qualifications. It is only by considering how we can best meet the needs of teacher trainees that we can begin to address the hidden struggles and frustrations they face in trying to meet expectations of an assessment strategy that does not serve them or the training providers as well as it should.

References

Cunningham, B. (2005) *Mentoring Teachers in Post Compulsory Education: A guide to Effective Practice*. London: David Fulton Publishers.

Peterson, K. (1994) NCREL Monograph. *Building Collaborative Cultures: Seeking Ways to Re-shape Urban Schools*. Available at www.ncrel.org/sdrs/areas/issues/ecucatrs/leadrshp/leOpetr.htm Accessed on February 10, 2009.

Shain, F. (1998) *Changing Notions of Teacher Professionalism in the Further Education Sector*. Presented at The British Educational Research Association Annual Conference, Queens University August 1998. Available at www.leeds.ac.uk/educol/documents/000000939.htm Accessed on February 21, 2009.

Schön, D. (1983) *The Reflective Practitioner*. New York: Basic Books.

Daring to teach teachers: Passion, politics and philosophy in post-compulsory teacher education

Debbie Bentley

…the classroom remains the most radical space of possibility in the academy.

(hooks, 1994:12)

My passion for philosophy and politics began in earnest many years ago in the early nineties when I was a new lecturer teaching a group of undergraduate Education Studies students at a new university. I remember very clearly two instances where my own perception of my role as an 'unofficial' Teacher Educator was somewhat at odds with the general consensus. The first, I asked a group of first year students to consider what they thought of Barry Troyna's (1985) statement 'Conflict and division arise not out of difference but from denial of the right to be different'. I was taken off this team taught module the following week and quietly informed that '*we shouldn't be so political*'. At this point it is worth noting that the title of the set assignment was 'Education is a political football. Discuss'. The second involved being less quietly reprimanded for exploring the works of Paulo Friere, Ivan Illich, John Gatto, Carl Rogers and John Holt, amongst others, within a module entitled 'Teacher Socialisation'. The inappropriateness of my approach was explained very clearly: '*these students are going to become teachers, we shouldn't be teaching them this stuff*'.

It was becoming increasingly apparent to me that within this particular degree programme I would not be allowed to expose any potential teachers to the kinds of political and philosophical works which other 'academic' undergraduates were encouraged to consider. I can't imagine the response had I introduced Karl Marx, I didn't stay long enough!

I have now been an 'official' teacher educator (post-compulsory) in colleges for over ten years. In that time I have found the culture of further education far more conducive to helping teachers consider their practice based upon a developing awareness of the value of a critical professionalism. I will never forget Pete, an engineering teacher who had come into teaching through industry, who had never been to college himself and stated in his interview '*I'm not good at this, I've never really read a book, even at school*'. Pete charged into my office one day waving Friere's '*Pedagogy of the Oppressed*'. '*This is it*', he shouted, '*this is everything, this is me, this is my students!*' He went on to cite Friere in every piece of work for the entirety of the course. And Sheila, who in class one day exclaimed to all, '*my curriculum is racist*!', to the astonishment of both herself and her colleagues.

My own philosophy and that of the teacher education team with which I work, is very much based upon developing 'authentic' practice, as defined by Kreber *et al.* (2007: 24):

> *…To make individuals more whole, more integrated, more fully human, more content with their personal and professional lives, their actions more clearly linked to purpose, 'empowered', better able to engage in community with others, and so forth.*

In practical terms, the team seek to create environments conducive to generating greater authenticity amongst teachers. As Brouwer and Korthagen (2005) suggest, educational change is also our cherished ideal. This is not always easy in a higher education sector criticised for it's over emphasis on the rational mind and subsequent failure to engage the *'hearts and spirits'* of its participants, (Kreber *et al.*, 2007; hooks, 2003; Vince, 1996). Often the *'freedom to create and to construct, to wonder and to venture'* (Friere, 1972: 32) is severely restricted by the *'various ideological and material conditions within [our] institutions'* (Zeichner and Gore, 1990: 343).

So what are the philosophical and political tensions for teacher educators attempting to build a culture of authenticity? Delivering a university franchised Certificate/ Post Graduate in Education (Post-Compulsory) has facilitated the development of programmes of study which have accommodated and supported both the culture and philosophy of the college and its teacher education team. However, the validation of a new programme designed explicitly to meet the new SVUK (Standard Verification UK) standards, and certainly influenced by the new quality assurance agenda in teacher education, has presented particular challenges in that:

> *Such programmes publicly claim to value students' experiential knowledge, and to give them specific tools to gain more control over their work lives, whilst simultaneously nullifying any sense of control through the way their learning is assessed.*

> (Elliott, 2008: 289)

Our teachers, many of whom are in-service, are accustomed to a certain level of authority in their professional lives based upon their knowledge and experience. If this knowledge and experience is not attributed value and worth within the curriculum and assessment processes teachers can often feel disempowered and become resistant, adopting a passive neutral voice, (Pavlovich *et al.*, 2009), and subsequently a surface approach to their learning.

In response to these concerns and after much consideration of the ethical agenda of our assessment philosophy and practice, (Smart and Dixon, 2002), the teacher training team decided to introduce a change in the assessment strategy for a collaborative observation project. The teachers work in small groups, documenting their experience in a journal which is not part of the overall grade but is intended to inform the summative assessment, a 3,000 word individual essay (with a 30% weighting of the overall mark) reflecting upon the experience. We decided to pilot a group viva as an alternative assessment strategy.

Given the philosophy of the collaborative project and the underpinning principles of authenticity, critical reflection and community, we felt a group viva (30-45 minutes, videoed for grading and moderation purposes) would provide a more fitting vehicle for teachers to truly engage with the process of learning. Gibb's (1995: 31) statement echoes our own experience:

> *...If the assessment consists of an individual report then students have no incentive to take teamwork seriously and will concentrate on private, competitive study.*

The importance, and difficulty, of modelling authentic practice in ensuring that assessment supports development is also discussed by Baldwin (2007: 5) who comments:

> *If we want learners to focus on, and value, learning, rather than the results of that learning as measured by marks, then we, as educators, need to look more closely at the environment which we create for our learners...and the role that we allow assessment to play in this.*

The groups were supported through an initial 'mock' group viva, designed to introduce the process, build confidence and provide further guidance for the formal assessment. We deliberated at length on the appropriateness of chairing or leading the group viva, essentially to provide structure for groups we felt may lack focus in addressing the assessment criteria. Ultimately, we felt that in this case our involvement would serve to undermine rather than support the development of our teachers' abilities to take responsibility for themselves and each other in the learning process.

Drawing upon Dewey's (1955) principle of *'democratic faith'*, and Van Manen's (1997) concept of *'mindfulness'*, we envisaged that the group viva would potentially provide *'a moment of transformation'* (Friere, 1972) as:

> *discussion at its best exemplifies the democratic process...incorporating reciprocity and movement, exchange and enquiry, cooperation and collaboration, formality and informality...through which a collective wisdom emerges that would have been impossible for any of the participants to achieve on their own.*
>
> (Brookfield and Preskill, 1999: 5)

As assessors we felt we could have no legitimate role in a process through which we proposed to *'honour...the teachers' priorities, visions and contexts'* (Coffey *et al.*, 2005: 182). A list of questions was created, based upon the assessment criteria, which participants could select from to help focus and structure the discussion. Groups were handed this list prior to the start of the formal assessment and allowed five minutes to discuss. Participants were also encouraged to use their journals throughout the process.

According to Abrami (1995) collegial working which involves an exploration of personal constructs is a preparation for controversy, empowering individuals to discuss, argue, negotiate and accept another. The group viva encourages teachers to demonstrate, explore and develop their skills in this area. These skills are becoming increasingly important in counteracting the:

> *growing trend (internationally) to prescribe teachers' and teacher educators' work...in a society where standardisation and prescription are being mistaken for higher standards.*
>
> (Cochran Smith, 2001: 4)

Drawing upon Elliott's (2008) account of how collaborative assessment methods can at least lead to a '*repositioning of the student's experience*' in which the assessment experience itself becomes '*a source for knowledge*', the group viva has been designed to encourage teachers '*to consider how they interact with the content rather than solely on what the content is*' (Pavlovich et al., 2009) and thus provide '*a means by which they can evaluate their own learning*' (Smart and Dixon, 2002: 193).

The teacher education team sought to create an environment in which teachers were supported and challenged to explore and develop authentic practice based upon a critically reflective approach and in this regard the introduction of the group viva has been a great success. Only three of our sixty teachers failed to demonstrate their achievement of the assessment criteria through the group viva, and indeed the majority of students not only surpassed our expectations with regard to their level of self awareness, creativity, sensitivity and imagination in working with the course material, but their enthusiasm for and enjoyment of the group viva process was heartening. At no point in my teaching career so far have student evaluations identified the assessment strategy as the '*best part of the module!*' In addition, a colleague who has worked on this module for over eight years stated that for her the new assessment strategy '*has breathed new life into the process*'.

However, negotiating the sharing of the group viva initiative with colleagues in colleges across our partnership has highlighted our different perceptions of the role and purpose of assessment, particularly in the present political climate, reflecting the wider debates which question the purpose, usefulness and value of what is assessed, why and for whom.

The wider partnership of colleges with whom we collaborate operates as a community of practice where teacher educators attempt to work democratically in ensuring high quality, relevant and theoretically informed teacher education. Whilst we share this common purpose, however, we do not necessarily share the same philosophical beliefs. As Richardson (1990: 9) reminds us:

> *To be involved in education… is to be involved in politics and politicking - in jockeying and negotiating for power and autonomy, and in manoeuvres to resist the power, threats and intrigues of others.*

Our competing philosophies reflect the contradictions inherent in recent education policy. Attempts to balance a philosophy based upon organisational autonomy and quasi-markets with a model comprising centrally established targets, mandatory planning, performance management and inspection (Hoggett, 1996) has resulted in a move towards:

> *an impoverished conception of purpose within education that reifies outcomes that can be measured over others that are more elusive but valuable.*
>
> (Simpkins, 2005: 13)

Elliott (2008) and Boud and Walker (1998) provide a clear example of the dangers of such a move in their criticism that familiar understandings of reflection in experiential learning contexts, particularly when forming part of an assessment strategy as in this case, are often simplistic and approaches overly instrumental, focusing upon *'technicist prescriptions'* and problem solving rather than what Van Manen (1997) describes as *'resolution through deeper understanding'*.

Drawing upon Serafini's (2000) work, Falchikov (2005) suggests that current policy promotes multiple concepts of assessment which serve different purposes, although all are focused primarily upon monitoring the work of teachers and teacher educators. The *'assessment as enquiry'*, model upon which our initiative is based, (also described as authentic, autonomous, transformative, participative and dynamic, valuing processes rather than products), challenges other models which emphasise the requirements of external regulation and standardisation rather than the learning experience.

Being well aware of Gramsci's (2000) assertion that each of us is accountable for the role we play (or fail to play) in the larger struggles of the day, our discussions in the partnership revolve around the extent to which we allow ourselves to become a *'carefully cultivated and contained ornament'* (Richardson, 1990), or alternatively demand nothing less than the *'freedom to create and to construct, to wonder and to venture'* (Friere, 1972). Wherever these discussions take us it is essential that teacher educators grapple with such issues of authenticity and take the lead in finding ways to confront the truth (Zimmerman, 1986), rather than slipping into the comfortable routine of *'everydayness'* (Heidegger, 1962). Cranton (2001) echoes Grimmet and Neufeld (1994) in arguing that teacher authenticity is fundamental to the moral development of our profession. Teacher educators need to be vigilant and support other teachers in adopting *'recognitive approaches'* which focus upon the centrality of socially democratic processes in working towards social justice for which self identity, self respect, self development, self expression and self determination are key conditions (Gale and Densmore, 2000).

As Friere (1972) argues, the path to liberation comes through critical awareness of one's reality and neither teachers nor teacher educators are exempt. Teachers can become active subjects of their own destiny only when they are truly in control of their practice. Practicing authentically may mean that boundaries of convention must sometimes be transgressed in order to critically engage with reality and eventually transform it, but it is only by doing so that teacher educators truly act as change agents and support teachers in developing their own authentic practice.

> *Such a choice is demanded of [all] teachers in relation to the power structures of the education system as well as to those of society. Therefore a major purpose of all in-service training programmes and staff development activities should be to enable this choice to be clarified and made. Teachers in their turn [can then] help their students in such choosing…Certainly it seems idle to promote 'a world community' or 'democratic and participatory society' without seeking to bring these concepts alive.*
>
> (Richardson, 1990: 122)

As teacher educators we tread a delicate and uneasy line between institutional pressure and the need for our own authentic development and practice and we can often feel uncomfortable, vulnerable and disempowered by educational contexts which represent and replicate external social power relations. These can undermine our knowledge, experience and authority and present real risks to our material wellbeing, career prospects and reputation. We must ensure that we do not distance ourselves from our own authenticity, or even negate the efforts of those seeking to develop and promote an authentically critical professionalism based upon the principles of democracy and social justice, as this will ultimately serve to undermine not only our own development but that of our colleagues, profession and learners (Gibbs 1995).

> *Each individual is unique and has her own distinct unfolding. But also all are members of groups, collectives and communities…Therefore the futures of collective identities are at stake in education, not those of individuals only.*
>
> (Richardson, 1990: 3)

To conclude, a short tale will serve to echo the theme of this chapter. A few years ago whilst searching through the shelves in a second hand book shop I came across Robin Richardson's profound text 'Daring to be a Teacher', a collection of essays based upon his experiences as a teacher and advisor in Brent and Berkshire during the 1980s. An inscription on the front inside cover read:

> *To Jenny, whether or not you dare, you will find much wisdom, wit and inspiration in these pages to help you on the threshold of your career. Congratulations on your graduation and much love, Mum and Dad (July 1991).*

Jenny's Mum and Dad had selected for their daughter not Reece and Walker's (2007) mechanistic 'Teaching, Training and Learning', or even Cowley's (2001) 'Getting the Buggers to Behave', but Richardson's reflections on the teacher's need to develop a passion for educational politics and philosophy which would underpin her practice with a sense of purpose, and serve to enthuse and energise in good times, whilst sustaining, encouraging and providing a sense of hope in those which are more '*hazardous*' and when '*great daring is required of us*' (Richardson 1990: 8).

References

Abrami, P. C., Chambers, B., Poulsen, C., De Simone, C., d'Apollonia, S. and Howden, J. (1995). *Classroom connections: Understanding and using co-operative learning*. Harcourt Brace.

Baldwin, L. (2007) *Editorial, Active Learning in Higher Education* 8: 5-8.

Boud, D. and Walker, D. (1998) *Promoting Reflection in Professional Courses: The Challenge of Context, Studies in Higher Education 23* (2): 191-206.

Brookfield, S. and Preskill, S. (1999) *Discussion as a Way of Teaching. Society for Research into Higher Education.*

Brouwer, N. and Korthagen, F. (2005) *Can Teacher Education Make a Difference? American Educational Research Journal 4* : 1: 153-224.

Cochran Smith, M. (2001) *Teacher Education at the Turn of the Century, Journal of Teacher Education.* 51: 163-165.

Coffey, J., Sato, M. and Thiebault, M. (2005) *Classroom Assessment Up Close - and personal, Teacher Development 9*: 2: 169-184.

Cowley, S. (2001) *Getting the Buggers to Behave*, (3rd edn). Continuum.

Cranton, P. A. (2001) *Becoming and Authentic Teacher in Higher Education*. Krieger.

Dewey, J. (1955) *Democracy and education. An introduction to the philosophy of education*. The Macmillan Company.

Elliott, C. (2008) Emancipating Assessment: Assessment Assumptions and Critical Alternatives in an Experience-based Programme. *Management Learning 39*: 271-293.

Falchikov, N. (2005) *Improving Assessment Through Student Involvement*. Routledge Falmer.

Friere, P. (1972) *Pedagogy of the Oppressed*. Penguin Books.

Gale, T. and Densmore, K. (2000) *Just schooling: Explorations in the cultural politics of teaching*. Open University Press.

Gibbs, G. (1995) *Learning in Teams: a Tutor Guide*. Oxford Centre for Staff Development.

Gramsci, A. (2000) *A Gramsci Reader: Selected Writings 1916-1935*, Schocken.

Grimmet, P. and Neufeld, J. (Eds) (1994) *Teacher development and the struggle for authenticity. Professional growth and restructuring in the context of change.* Teachers College Press.

Heidegger, M. (1962) Being and Time, in: M. Zimmerman, (1986) *The development of Heidegger's concept of authenticity. Eclipse of the self*. Ohio University Press.

Hoggett, P. (1996) *New Models of Control in the Public Service. Public Administration. 74*: 9-32.

hooks, b. (1994) *Teaching to transgress: Education as the practice of freedom.* Routledge.

hooks, b. (2003) *Teaching community. A pedagogy of hope.* Routledge.

Kreber, C., Klampfleitner, M., McCune, V., Bayne, S. and Knottenbelt, M. (2007) What do You Mean by 'Authentic'? A Comparative Review of the Literature on Conceptions of Authenticity in Teaching, *Adult Education Quarterly 58:* 22-43.

Pavlovich, K., Collins, E. and Jones, G. (2009) Developing Students' Skills in Reflective Practice: Design and Assessment, *Journal of Management Education 33:* 37-58.

Reece, I. and Walker, S. (2007) *Teaching, Training and Learning: A Practical Guide* (6th edn). Business Education Publisher.

Richardson, R. (1990) *Daring to be a Teacher*. Trentham Books

Serafini, F. (2000) Three Paradigms of Assessment: Measurement, Procedure and Enquiry. *The Reading Teacher.* 54: 384-393.

Simpkins, T. (2005) Leadership in Education: 'What Works' or 'What Makes Sense', *Educational Management Administration Leadership: 33* (1) 9-16.

Smart, J. and Dixon, S. (2002) The Discourse of Assessment: Language and Value in the Assessment of Group Practice in the Performing Arts, *Arts and Humanities in Higher Education 1:* 185-204.

Troyna, B. and Williams, J. (1985) *Racism, Education and the State*, Croom Helm.

Van Manen, M. (1997) *Researching lived experience*. Althouse Press.

Vince, R. (1996) Experiential Management Education as the Practice of Change, in: R. French and C. Grey (Eds) *Rethinking Management Education*. Sage.

Zeichner, K. and Gore, J. (1990) Teacher Socialisation, W. R. Housten, (Ed.) *Handbook of Research on Teacher Education*. Macmillan.

Zimmerman, M. (1986) *The development of Heidegger's concept of authenticity. Eclipse of the self.* Ohio University Press.

'Action research or research in action'

Karen Lowe

My role as the Head of a School of Education in a large Pennine Lancashire College brings many responsibilities. As a manager I have to meet the dual challenges of leading a team and a department but also as a teacher educator, who has teaching and learning at their very core, it is underpinned by my own ambition to inspire, develop and even challenge those studying on Initial Teacher Training programmes. Whilst some of the learners are pre-service others may have been working in the hugely diverse post compulsory sector for many years and their approach to research, Continuing Professional Development (CPD), and the critical analysis of links between theory and practice, can vary from enthusiasm and hunger to apathy, disillusionment , or at its most extreme, hostility. It is against this backdrop that I am professionally directed and personally motivated to support and sustain an active engagement with the development of learning using research, reflection and action as an investment of time.

For many people research is something that other people do. Clever people, 'boffins' important erudite people who work on large-scale commissioned activity which results in publications and very often draws national attention and commentary. Research viewed in this way is for people who have nothing better to do as it is time consuming; the assumption is that ordinary hard working people with busy lives to lead don't have time for it. However, research is not one thing and many practitioners have used action research to support their own professional practice and development. Rather than large-scale commissioned research, which can sometimes be divorced from practice, it starts with the teacher and the learner. The questions come directly from practice and the 'results' underpin change and development producing a new cycle of reflection and questions. Action research is no less challenging or demanding but it is the *'combination of action and research that has contributed to its attraction to researchers, teachers and educational community alike, demolishing Hodgkinson's (1957) corrosive criticism of action research as easy hobby games for little engineers'* (in Cohen *et al.*, 2003: 226-227).

In my career I worked with Health and Social Care students who undertook work placements in a variety of settings. Apart from the logistics of organisation, health and safety demands, and the practical elements of working with a range of service providers, the biggest issues centred on trying to match students requests with suitable, available placements. As a relatively new tutor I wanted to meet individual requests such as:

> *I want to go to a school. Don't send me to an old peoples' home. I can't do that...old people frighten me...adults who can't talk properly, are scary...small children are lovely get me in a nursery.*

Experience taught me that this matching exercise was unrealistic and that it could be unproductive, defeating the very philosophy and values which underpinned the ethos of 'Working in Placement' modules. Every student was therefore placed in a variety of settings during the course of their studies. Careful planning and preparation took place before the students left the classroom, time was dedicated to supporting them during their working experience and evaluation of learning was built into the sessions following their return. It became apparent that although these experiences often confirmed the learners' earlier thoughts, in a number of cases it actually caused them to reconsider their earlier opinions. For example:

> *Small children make so much noise...they wet themselves and have snotty noses...old people are brilliant they talk and have so much to share...watching an adult with a learning difficulty buy something at the shop made me feel proud.*

The learners were now able to make informed career choices. By determining what they thought the issues were, by exploring them through active participation and by formulating how this had affected their existing behaviours and future intentions, they had been part of a research activity. Students had predetermined that there were issues around working in certain environments, experienced these on work placement and then reflected on whether they were actually correct or if the data and information they had collected had proved them correct or was misdirected in their views. The information would not only help them make informed career choices but could also be used to shape the future practice of other learners, tutors and possibly even service providers.

This had a major impact on my approach to research; the part it plays in personal and professional activity and how, if considered and conducted with care, the benefits can be phenomenal. No amount of theory can replace the integrated approach of planning, carrying out, evaluating, concluding and reflecting, and by taking a holistic approach perhaps all those engaged in it, either novices or more experienced, can enjoy the enhanced opportunities and strengthened experiences it brings.

The demand for staff to record their own CPD grows. External influences such as Integrated Quality Enhancement Reviews ask for this. The Institute for Learning (IfL) require evidence of it, and employers striving to meet Teaching Quality Standards reinforce its importance. Those who feel pressured just doing their job, question the validity and purpose of extra activity which they see as peripheral. Is action research one such challenge or could it be reframed to be 'research in action', and what are the issues which impact on those trying to encourage and support, to empower their colleagues to embrace this?

This reticence is overt amongst the teams I work with and it is this culture which has led me to critically reflect on the way I see research and to consider strategies to try to manage those who view the idea of undertaking any type of research with trepidation and very often open resistance.

'*Have you any idea how busy I am?*' is a common response, and it is this which has caused me to look at the way we approach research, the value of action research and ways to emphasise the potential positive relationship between this type of activity and the very best professional practice. By encouraging the critical analysis of research and embracing the relevance of it to practice could it be less threatening?

In order to reflect on this it seems appropriate to give my own research skills attention and to look towards analysing the significance of study in my own professional life. Although I have been teaching for many years it is important that I reflect upon my own CPD as new entrants are now required to do. The journey of professional formation, ultimately leading to the award of Qualified Teacher Learning and Skills (QTLS) or Associate Teacher Learning and Skills (ATLS) will reinforce the continual assessment of teachers against occupational standards and this will not be limited to time (IfL, 2009).

It was at this stage that I realised I needed to try to identify more clearly the ideas that I was forming, and that if I was to engage with the concepts in a structured way I would need more than my own thoughts to support potential change. I made space to meet with my colleagues to collect information on the activities which 'shout the loudest' during their working life and which potentially preclude them from following through the 'whispers' which they would really like to explore. They welcomed an opportunity to articulate this and none of the issues raised were new or surprising. What did become apparent however was the breadth of activity being undertaken and accepted by motivated practitioners. They demonstrated a shared passion for their job which allowed them to speak with pride about their commitment to all the elements of teaching and learning which they clearly saw as nothing 'out of the ordinary.'

Using this information I brought together a diary of daily entries that a typical teaching day could bring and decided to consider if this very descriptive data could be used to generate more evaluative analysis.

8am	Staff meeting to discuss new timetables for additional school group. Some people not too keen on working with this type of student. 15 year olds bring so many complications and we're not a school after all.
9am	First class of the day - entry level group and they don't get going for at least 10 minutes. They are young and they should have so much energy at that age but the first part is either 'flat' or chaotic.
9.50am	Break - speak to late student about potential impact of actions. Record on register and follow curriculum centre policy.
10.00am	Continue class - manage difficult group dynamics. Sulky student.
11.00am	Rush to next session - just in time.
12.00am	Lunch time - complete risk assessment for trip - is it worth it! Chat with colleagues about delay in EMA payments, and how to fit an extra desk in the staff room for the new tutor. Reminisce about our own 'first day' and laugh about it. (Wise old owls now!)
1.00pm	The post lunch slot - Students full of food and they can be quite lethargic. I find this a hard slot as well.
2.30pm	Break time - ring Disability Officer and Student Counsellor to check availability.
2.40pm	NVQ portfolio building session. Vocational students time in college to do the 'dull bit'.
4pm	Look forward to this class - workshop in the studio and even though it's a huge group there is support from colleagues and technicians. The whole room is busy and active - despite the radio, the lack of space, the wobbly board and the lateness in the day.
6pm	The group should have gone by now but there are always some who want to hang behind and keep me from my tea. I am happy to answer questions but am aware that it is parents evening. Find 5 minutes to ring my own children and remind them that I will be late home.
6.15pm	Late for parents evening - catch up all night. Haven't eaten anything all day so feeling tired and irritable.
8pm	Time to go home at last. Lessons to prepare for tomorrow and handouts to photocopy. Tomorrows Diploma group are applying for University and suddenly they seem to feel an urgency to get on with things. Why have they waited so long?
8.15pm	Almost there - just made it to the car park and dodged my manager. I've got a horrible feeling she is going to ask me to do some action research thing. Not a chance - I don't want to be collared for that when I am this busy.

There is nothing fictitious about this sort of demanding day and it reflects the changes in the role of those working in a taxing and challenging sector. The days where teachers could sit in a classroom, close the door and look forward to the 'Italian Job' car park dash at the end of the day with the dreams of long holidays, have gone, if they ever existed. Nevertheless the perceived perceptions of teaching and learning being an undemanding profession perhaps remain whilst the reality is that those working in the sector are committed and dedicated, yet they can feel increasingly exposed and vulnerable. Reflection can be seen as defensive rather than pro active and the tendency is to consider critical incidents and turning points as negative experiences rather than more positive ones.

It is perhaps no surprise then that comments from staff reflect what they perceive as the ever increasing demands of things which they see as additional to their 'proper job'. In this climate as managers, personnel departments, professional bodies, and changing requirements within the sector teacher educators increasingly ask for evidence of CPD. The relevance of research is not always seen positively. One staff member told me '*I'm too busy for that stuff, leave it to the experts*' which caused me to look at how I approach research, how I present the concept to colleagues and whether I am guilty of perpetuating the belief that it is 'done' out there, by others. In my example mentioned at the start of this chapter, I am happy to call what I did research and yet there was no mention of quantitative data, structured or semi structured interviews, questionnaire design, Likert scales, rating and ranking and no attempt to input the data into statistical packages. There was no reference to longitudinal, cross-sectional or trend studies, no discussion of reliability or validity and no attempt to explain correlation or significance (Bell and Opie, 2002). This raises the question of what counts as research and whether what I did would be called research by others. The results clearly impacted upon practice but would it be accepted as research? This raises the question of whether all research has to follow the same guidelines, criteria and procedures before it can be accepted or called research.

Action research challenges the scientific definition of research which is distinguished by empirical observation, a clear hypothesis and uses data and theory to determine facts and evidence which should prove or disprove an initial statement. Findings are substantiated by data and figures and these can be interpreted and translated to support statements and give answers. Action research is defined by other characteristics. It is not something done to others by the researchers, indeed the researcher is an active participant. It is collaborative and centres on reflection, evaluation and some would argue that optimistically, it leads to positive change for all engaged in it.

Could this be used to change how professional people and those aspiring to develop their own knowledge and understanding, look at their own daily activities? Could this broader interpretation lead to a host of opportunities, which, with only minimal adjustments, could meet all the criteria to define them as action research? I think on reflection I used action research in my own practice before I knew what it was called.

If this approach can be used to change the way that our teaching activities are perceived the results could be phenomenal. This shift in attitude could help research opportunities to be identified, rather than manufactured, and their contribution would seamlessly become integral and complementary rather than additional.

I started to reconsider the typical teaching day mentioned above and wondered if there were questions this raised and if these questions could then be the catalysts for action research. To show the research opportunities I have added an additional column to the existing grid.

		Action Research Opportunity
8am	Staff meeting to discuss new timetables for additional school group. Some people not too keen on working with this type of student. 15 year olds bring so many complications and we're not a school after all.	*What has led to school groups attending College?* *What are the challenges /differences when working with 15 year olds?* *Do the groups like being here?* *How can we make a difference?*
9am	First class of the day - entry level group and they don't get going for at least 10 minutes. They are young and they should have so much energy at that age but the first part is either 'flat' or chaotic.	*Does timing of sessions impact on concentration?* *How can I design the introductory phase of my teaching sessions to meet learner needs?*
9.50am	Break - speak to late student about potential impact of actions. Record on register and follow curriculum centre policy. Why is lateness an issue?	*What strategies can we use to combat lateness and are some more effective than others?*
10.00am	Continue class - manage difficult group dynamics. Sulky student.	*Why do some learners remain disengaged? How does this affect group dynamics?*
11.00am	Rush to next session - just in time.	*Should we review timetables to value all the working day - not just the class sessions?*
12.00am	Lunch time - complete risk assessment for trip - is it worth it! Chat with colleagues about delay in EMA payments, and how to fit an extra desk in the staff room for the new tutor. Reminisce about our own 'first day' and laugh about it.	*What is the value of educational visits? Does this enhance teaching and learning? Is it more effective to bring the subject to the classroom or take the classroom to the subject?* *Do first impressions count?* *Do financial incentives affect retention/achievement/motivation?*
1.00pm	The post lunch slot - Students full of food and they can be quite lethargic. I find this a hard slot as well.	*What is the impact of timing? What are the links between physiology, psychology and learning?*
2.30pm	Break time - ring disability officer and student counsellor to check availability.	*Student support. What is it and how can it enhance retention, achievement, teaching and learning?*

2.40pm	NVQ portfolio building session. Vocational students time in college to do the 'dull bit.'	*Theory and practice - how can links be strengthened?* *Do preferred learning styles have a part to play for learners, tutors and courses or is it just common sense?*
4pm	Look forward to this class - workshop in the studio and even though it's a huge group there is support from colleagues and technicians. The whole room is busy and active - despite the radio, the lack of space, the wobbly board and the lateness in the day.	*What impact does environment have?* *Does music enhance the teaching experience or act as a distraction?* *Is simulation a valid tool?*
6pm	The group should have gone by now but there are always some who want to hang behind and keep me from my tea. I am happy to answer questions but am aware that it is parents evening. Find 5 minutes to ring my own children and remind them that I will be late home.	*Should tutorial sessions be redesigned?* *Should teaching sessions be resigned to accommodate plenary activities which answer questions?*
6.15pm	Late for parents evening - catch up all night. Haven't eaten anything all day so feeling tired and irritable.	*What are the psychological barriers to teaching and learning?* *Is there a link between diet and behaviour?*
8pm	Time to go home at last. Lessons to prepare for tomorrow and handouts to photocopy. Tomorrow's Diploma group are applying for University and suddenly they seem to feel an urgency to get on with things. Why have they waited so long?	*How does the structure of a programme of study need to adapt over the year? Do changes reflect the significant issues of induction to progression and the development of higher level skills?*
8.15pm	Almost there - just made it to the car park and dodged my manager. I've got a horrible feeling she is going to ask me to do some action research thing. Not a chance –I don't want to be collared for that when I am this busy.	*How can managers reframe perceptions and what is the value of doing this.* ***Is it action research or research in action?***

Research in action

In thinking about what research is and how it can support critical reflection for teachers I can see the benefit of action research as this is clearly linked to practice and to creating change; both in the ways that we see things as well as in the actual practice that we carry out. Whilst I can see this benefit myself as a manager I am interested in supporting this development in others. This has led me to think about how action research can be used as a tool to support research in action - that is the action of teaching and learning. I question whether if explained in this way it may have more significance for busy practitioners who do not want any more management burdens placed upon them, even well-meaning CPD burdens.

Whilst writing this chapter I can clearly see the development of ideas of research in action shaping into concrete plans for future development. Change is likely to take time and may need a much more structured form, but this is not the end of a reflective process, rather the inspiration for future development. Reflection is already leading to a personal change in attitude and this is being transferred both personally and professionally to colleagues and learners. My roles continue to raise questions about practical matters such as planning, timetabling, attendance and retention but now instead of merely trying to manage these and react to the most pressing elements, I actively try to work backwards and try to identify the real issues. One course has already received fewer applications than at this time last year. It is not enough to try to advertise and get more students enrolled; it is more meaningful and more useful to try to find out why there has been a change? It seems strange that the very act of considering research as an agent for change has inspired planning for research. Practical adjustments have been to encourage and support research activity and strategies are in place to evaluate the effectiveness of these changes. This will take the form of quantitative and qualitative data and whilst this may not 'change the world' it may impact on a small, but equally as important part of it. Managers have built space into timetables to allow remission hours to be available for those who would like to undertake research. This is a genuine investment which reflects the belief that such enterprises will not only benefit individuals but that the findings can also be important for colleagues, learners and the organisation. A research committee is to be formed but this will not be led by a champion of research but rather it will be a genuinely collaborative group who will work together to support the development of activity which will be recorded and shared. This is not to be exclusive but rather it is being promoted as an integral element of best practice, a space to share but more importantly this group is to be a catalyst for action. Whist reports are to be produced and their findings are to be valued, most of all they are to be accessible. This forum will not merely create research it will distribute the very best investigations which professional practitioners are undertaking through their daily activity and working lives. Recognising the research which is going on, recording this, cascading and valuing it, has gradually become as important as initiating it. In its infancy this may be a gentle breeze rather than a wind of change but this will certainly be measured and reviewed following the first year and I have no doubt that it will start a process which will feed into future planning cycles. This will indeed be *'small scale intervention in the functioning of the real world'* followed by *'a close examination of the effects of such an intervention'* (Cohen *et al.*, 2003: 227) and its potential is challenging yet exciting.

Fawbert (2003: 22) argues that *'Reflective action...involves a willingness to engage in constant self appraisal and development'* and from this beginning action research can be formulated and followed through. Over past weeks I have been exploring not only the dynamic world of education, my own organisation and those working in it, but most importantly my own beliefs. It has been satisfying to make time to really consider the questions this reflection has raised and to consider the future. Too often it is not that we are unwilling to engage in this type of deliberate contemplation, but rather we are not able to prioritise this above other things. The very act of making this a priority for me has been a personal challenge, but an investment by me, in myself, and a precursor of what is still to come. As Bryant argued:

> In action research and reflective practice, perhaps the most important message is that there is always more to be said.
>
> (Bryant in Scott and Usher, 1996: 119)

References

Bell, J. and Opie, C. (2002) *Learning from Research*. Buckingham: Open University. Press.

Cohen, L., Manion, L. and Morrison, K. (2003) *Research Methods in Education*, (5th edn). London: Routledge Falmer.

Fawbert, F. (Ed.) (2003) *Teaching in Post-Compulsory Education*. London: Continuum.

Hodgkinson, H. L. (1957) *Action Research - a critique, Journal of Educational Sociology*, 31 (4).

Institute for Learning, *Licence to Practice: Professional Formation. A guide to QTLS and ATLS status*. Institute for Learning. London.

Scott, D. and Usher, R. (1996) *Action Research and Reflective Practice: Understanding Educational Research. London*: Routledge.

ITT observations and college quality assurance observations: The same but different? Is there a case for combining the two processes?

Duncan Crossland

Introduction

As the Manager of Adult and Higher Education in a large college in the North West of England I am responsible for the resource and curriculum management of a wide range of programmes. Central to these is a long running and very successful initial teacher training (ITT) course run in collaboration with a consortium of further education (FE) colleges and a university. Apart from being a popular course for trainees from a range of organisations involved in lifelong learning in the region it plays an important role in the college in terms of staff development, quality assurance and human resources.

While carrying out a recent observation of some members of my teaching team as part of our quality assurance (QA) process I became increasingly fascinated about the difference in approach between the QA model and the ITT model I had also worked with. In many colleges the two processes are entirely separate and ITT teams argue fiercely to maintain this separation and yet, while observing an adult education tutor who also happened to be on our Certificate /Post Graduate Certificate in Education (Cert Ed/PGCE) programme I could not resist asking why. In terms of consistency and managing heavy workloads I questioned why it was necessary for me to write up two separate observations of the same teaching session. And if I did, would there be any significant differences between the two reports and if not could the two reports be combined?

This was particularly pertinent as the issue of combining the two processes had been raised from time to time by college managers and fiercely resisted by the ITT team. This chapter explores why the two processes are seen as such different approaches to what superficially at least appears to be a common process of observing teaching.

This chapter also explores the differences between the two systems, in terms of their approach and function and competing notions of professionalism which underpin them. It goes on to examine what would have to change in order to bring the two approaches together. I reflect that only a radical change in the management of colleges and the role of ITT teams would enable this to happen.

Context

Recent changes in the regulations governing the programme and the introduction of Lifelong Learning UK (LLUK) standards have introduced radical changes to the ITT programme. In particular the increase in the minimum number of teaching observations per trainee to eight, including two by subject specialists, has raised issues about resourcing the programme which has impacted upon the relationship between the course and general college management. A simple response to the question of increased resourcing of teaching observations would be to link the purpose and recording of observations more closely allowing the utilisation of observation data already collected as part of the college's QA system or data gathered by the ITT team to be fed into the college system.

Combining of the QA and training responses appears unproblematic to many college managements and yet many ITT teams resist this approach. This may be because the main function of FE colleges is increasingly seen as tied to the economy, with training a management tool to grow the business rather than a vehicle for professional development. Colleges have always been connected with economic development. Callaghan's Ruskin College speech in 1976 is taken as a landmark for HE but the debate goes back further than that especially for the FE sector with roots in the Mechanics Institutes, the Workers' Educational Association (WEA) as well as in Technical Colleges. Currently the notion that FE is about employment and lifelong learning is akin to lifelong training for work goes largely unchallenged in terms of policy and funding. This unquestioned role may be in part why teacher educators are suspicious of moves to combine what they see as observations designed to support the development of teachers with a largely management tool designed to produce data for college purposes.

Similarities and differences between the processes

Superficially both processes share aspects in common. In particular this includes:

- Use of trained observers.

- Clear criteria for the assessment of the observation.

- Moderation process to ensure robustness.

There is also a high degree of agreement of the broad areas to be examined. Typically observers in both systems expect a well-planned session, use of appropriate methods and a well- managed session with judgements about the pace of the session, inclusiveness, use of resources and so on.

The degree of similarity between the systems can be seductive. However, there are important differences not least in the purpose and context of each system. The QA system is designed to assure the quality of the provision. Observations are therefore a sample of provision which when extrapolated assure college managements and external reviewers, notably the Office for Educational Standards (Ofsted), that the college in question is performing at a certain level and has a process which is robust enough to guarantee that any self-assessed grading of its activity is accurate. This has been characterised by O'Neill (2002) in the 2002 Reith Lecture as mere accountability, based on strengthened internal accountability, managerial approaches to quality assurance, lack of trust and an undermining of professional commitment in public services generally. It can be argued that this approach reduces reflection, innovative approaches and ultimately stifles the quality enhancement it is designed to encourage.

QA observation is based purely on the evidence as presented on that day. It is retrospective in nature and behaviourist in approach. It also strives to be quantitative rather than qualitative, providing management with percentages of outstanding or satisfactory grades. This frequently forms the basis of further targets to increase (or sometimes reduce if the results do not seem to support other data such as achievement or retention) in a bid to drive up quality. Such a quantitative approach relies on the ability to reproduce results over time and an attempt to pin down the activities of teaching and learning as a collection of reproducible actions.

There is a tension here as the new LLUK standards consist of around 200 statements which describe the activities of a teacher in the lifelong learning sector. The standards approach could be seen to a large extent to be an attempt to identify what is happening in one college and see how that college's performance compares with other institutions. As such it is thought to be value-free and objective but, as Silverman's (2004) discussion shows this may be illusory. If the definition of job roles in Silverman's example is to some extent subjective, how much more difficult is the process for defining good teaching in one simple grade required by Ofsted. The Standards have been introduced to support good practice but when this is accompanied by grading it has a financial as well as professional implication. It is possible that grade becomes an aim in itself, with FE staff reporting that they are relieved to be 'a Grade 1 teacher' or dread being branded a Grade 4 which will impact upon their professional identity as a good teacher and the college as a good institution.

ITT and professional value

This is in contrast with the typical criteria used in a university-validated scheme, where the emphasis is more clearly on concepts and knowledge. In this developmental model the process is more of a dialogue between professionals and the arriving at a judgement is a much more messy business than would be implied by the assignation of a simple number grade. For example, trainees are asked to 'consider' the learning environment (UCLan, 2008) and by implication make a professional judgement about how to exploit the state-of-the-art learning space or the cold temporary accommodation where even a flip chart is a luxury. In contrast the QA approach makes a judgement about the environment to produce useful data for management but treating the teacher as only one aspect of delivery while the training course focuses on the trainee teacher's development as a professional called upon to make professional judgements.

Hartzipanagos' and Lygo-Baker's study of the use of teaching observations is a largely positive account of the process which many ITT teams would recognise. It identifies critical reflection as a key positive outcome of the experience, summed up by the following statement from one of the participants who, after one or two observed sessions:

> ...*started to engage in critical reflection on my own teaching methods on my own...rather than solely when prompted by the teaching observer.*

(Hartzipanagos and Lygo-Baker, 2006: 427)

This is the outcome most teacher training programmes are designed to achieve. They do this by using well-designed tools such as reflective journals, pre-observation reflections and a well-structured programme involving short teaching experiences, group and individual discussion and course units designed to empower the trainee.

Competing notions of professionalism are at the heart of this tension between QA and ITT in relation to teaching observation. Most colleges would recognise the technical rational model, illustrated by the QA system, in contrast to the creative and interpretative model from ITT. This is shown in the following table contrasting the two models:

	Technical-Rational	Creative-Interpretive
Character	Technical, logical, convergent	Creative, interpretive, divergent
Focus	Economic progress	Personal well-being
People	As role occupants	Unique individual, agents
Capability	Solvable, convergent problems	'Messes', problematic solutions
Perspective	Solving problems, applying knowledge	Understanding problematic situations
Success Criteria	Logic, efficiency, cause-effect	Values, ethics, theory
Epistemology	Knowledge is stable and general	Knowledge is transient
Thinking	Logical, deductive	Inductive, uses intuition

Adapted from Martin *et al.*, (2007: 358)

The technical-rational approach is more likely to be concerned with prediction and control than with emancipation and freedom. An observation scheme based on this approach may thus reinforce the powerlessness of those without power (those being observed) and those with power (the observer). The observation situation itself reinforces the difference in power. The observer sits in the classroom, remains silent during the class and the teacher 'performs' knowing that their future may depend on how the observer interprets what is going on in this snapshot of an ongoing teaching and learning process. It would be naïve not to recognise that a power relationship also exists on teacher training courses but combining the two observation processes may heighten the power differential (see Nasta, 2007 for discussion on this).

Why colleges don't just adopt the ITT model

While there is no evidence that reinforcing power relations is the intention of college QA schemes, it may be their effect. Colleges need to manage a diverse portfolio of courses and are under external pressures to provide data. The technical-rational model sits well with the world in which colleges find themselves. Colleges are seen as central to the government's drive to up skill the population and improve the nation's economic performance. Targets are set - for example to increase the number of adults gaining full Level 2 and full Level 3 qualifications. This deficit model, which doesn't recognise the skills that people do have, identifies the source of failure at the level of the individual who can be 'repaired' and sent back into the workplace.

For those involved in education and particularly teacher education it is the attempt to limit education to a formulaic set of standards and targets which is most worrying. A technical-rationalist approach to teaching results in consistency which can soon turn to repetitiveness. Now every class begins with a list of objectives and ends with a re-visiting of them 'to check learning'. This approach is a sensible reaction to the apparently vague and unstructured sessions of some years ago, and it is one I have recommended to trainees struggling to make their sessions make sense to their learners. However, its constant use renders many sessions repetitive and predictable. FE lecturers know, however, that to vary from the model will result in a poor grade for the observation.

Some college targets add to this standardisation of learning experiences. Many colleges have a target for the use of information technology in lessons. This is interpreted as the use of smart boards, quizzes and games, which every session should now include. Achieving a 10% target for use of IT in the classroom, for example, is easier to measure than assessing the amount of deep learning occurring during the session, or later as result of it.

Creative-interpretive models, on the other hand, are difficult for FE managements to work with. They are based on difficult-to-measure data with all the problems of validity and reliability which that implies (see Cohen *et al.*, 2003: 117-133). For example, 'creative' solutions are not as simple to measure as achieving a target of X% Grade 1 observations. In a messy environment it is difficult to achieve the consistency that a quantitative approach to data demands. The fact that the individual learners change over time and between groups raises questions about the consistency of grades and what it is the grades are measuring. In part this difference is recognised by Ofsted as the new grading criteria for teacher training programmes are not the same as those used by colleges to assure quality. The Ofsted logic however breaks down even in its own terms by excluding new or trainee teachers from the process as if their performance is somehow not part of the overall performance of the college.

It is clear therefore that the two approaches are at odds with each other because of differences in their approach to data - quantitative versus qualitative, function and context. Is there any way forward or are the two sides going to continue to view each other suspiciously from their separate camps? Are teacher trainers right to remain suspicious of attempts to combine their observation system with the management process? Much of what has already been said would suggest they are. However, what would be the effect of such collaboration? Are there advantages for college managements beyond mere resource management? What are the positive possibilities for ITT teams interested in developing the expertise of trainees and staff generally?

Attempts to bring the two approaches together

Teacher trainers rightly resist attempts to ride rough-shod over their programmes but by refusing to engage in discussion with managements may be missing an opportunity to bring about real institutional change. In a genuine learning organisation the character of the QA observations would have to be very different, more akin to the teaching practice observations on ITT programmes. Although difficult this represents an opportunity for ITT teams to become more central to college management and to influence it in a way that reflects values and shifts colleges towards a truly learning organisation. Not that being a learning organisation is anything that colleges have not attempted or professed to be in the past. The concept of a learning organisation was very popular in business in the 1990s, a time following incorporation when colleges had what were seen as more pressing needs, including long-running disputes over employment contracts and a degree of bitterness which militated against an atmosphere of trust and openness essential to the development of more open management.

Nevertheless there have been recent attempts to move on and develop a new way of working. My own college re-visits its values regularly in a discussion which involves nearly all staff to some degree or another in 'Listen and Learn' sessions and focus groups for staff. National initiatives which could have supported this - and may well have in some instances - have been unfortunately couched in old-fashioned philosophies and a blame culture. Even during the disputes in the 1990s, new employment contracts typically included, for the first time, the provision of an identified number of days of Continuous Professional Development (CPD) for staff. This did not sit well with greatly increased teaching loads, in some cases with no limits, and there is little evidence that it resulted in any improvement in the development of teaching skills or subject knowledge.

A more recent example is the establishment of Subject Learning Coaches (SLCs) from 2002. Here was the gem of an idea which could have changed the culture of many colleges, establishing centres of expertise, even excellence, in teaching spearheaded by nationally trained SLCs supported by centrally produced high quality materials. However the initiative was seen as a response to the failure of FE to deliver high quality teaching as identified in 'Success for All' (DfES, 2002) supported by Ofsted reports of the failure of the system (HMSO, 2002). Brown *et al.* (2008) chart the good intentions of the scheme, with training of the SLCs to include collaborative working and cascading good practice between and within organisations.

The CPD requirement for FE lecturers is a beginning. Colleges have the opportunity to build this into a process which will inform and instigate change in the organisation. My own college already hosts a research conference where teams showcase research into curriculum development supported by the college's HE in FE funds and Teaching Quality Enhancement Fund. It has also appointed a HE Staff mentor whose role is to stimulate scholarly activity and bring genuine research-based curriculum development. Already some staff are piloting a scheme based on self-governing triads who will engage in peer observation and reflection on practice, in a similar way to the Cert Ed/PGCE 'Reflecting on Practice' module in the UCLan programme.

For a successful incorporation of ITT teaching observations into the general management of colleges there is a need for not just isolated examples but a significant change in management strategy towards a new model which may be akin to a learning organisation model or the innovative organisation described by Knowles (1990: 103) as *'people-centred...trusting'*, with a *'high tolerance of ambiguity'*, all qualities found in the creative interpretive model or reflected in initial teacher training programmes up and down the country. Given a change to this form of management the divide between ITT observations and the QA model would be much easier to bridge. ITT teams would become integral to a people-centred, adaptive institution based on collaborative decision making and a positive approach to problem solving.

A shift towards a new model would not be easy. Management theorists (for example Johnson and Scholes, 2002) describe strategic change as proceeding incrementally or in periods of flux with transformational change occurring only infrequently and often in response to environmental change. FE exists in a turbulent environment. It is easy to underestimate the degree of transformational change it has already undergone in recent years. Having learned to cope with the demands of the Learning and Skills Council (LSC) and Ofsted it is unlikely that colleges will be open to change in approach to management, and external demands would still have to be satisfied. Transformation into a learning organisation may be one step too far at present and representing risk to which managements do not wish to expose their organisations.

The uneasy relationship between the two approaches to teaching observations may unfortunately have to continue for the time being and there may never be a complete integration of the two systems into one approach. However the complete separation is arguably wasteful of resources and represents a missed opportunity for teacher educators to influence the development of the institutions in which they work. Incidentally, the adult education tutor did receive two separate reports and did well under both systems, but she was a competent teacher. A teacher with more development needs would test the ability to combine the two systems more thoroughly, but there is clearly a way forward here.

More substantial organisational change may typically be incremental and at times impossible but the very environment which has forced colleges to respond in the way they have may, by its very turbulence, cause another dramatic transformation in the management of FE. ITT teams will be aware of the dangers of becoming an arm of management, with their qualifications in danger of losing independence and therefore their currency in the wider world. Teacher education teams can continue to sit on the sidelines and watch on suspiciously or could cautiously and without compromising the values of their programmes work with college managements first of all to identify common needs and values. After all the two approaches have a common aim of supporting and developing a teaching force at the initial training stage and, increasingly through CPD, throughout teachers' careers. The problems should not be under-estimated but the prize is also great, nothing less than a transformation in values and practice in the further education system.

References

Brown, L., Kelly, J. and Sargent, D. (2008), Change or transformation? A critique of a nationally funded programme of Continuous Professional Development for the Further Education system, *Journal of Further and Higher Education 32*, no 4; 427-439.

Cohen, L., Manion, L. and Morrison, K. (2003) *Research Methods in Education*, (5th edn). London: Routledge and Farmer.

DfES (2002) *Success for All*. London: Department for Education and Skills.

Hartzipanagos, S. and Lygo-Baker, S. (2006) Teaching observations: promoting development through critical reflection, *Journal of Further and Higher Education 30*, no 4; 421-431.

HMSO (2002) *Report into the Findings of Her Majesty's Inspectorate: the state of Further Education*. London: Her Majesty's Stationery Office.

Johnson, G. and Scholes, K. (2002) *Exploring Corporate Strategy.* Edinburgh: Pearson Education Ltd.

Knowles, M. (1990) *The Adult Learner: A Neglected Species,* (4th edn). Houston: Gulf Publishing.

Martin, K., Summers, D. and Sjerps-Jones, H. (2007) Sustainability and Teacher Education, *Journal of Further and Higher Education 31*, no 4: 352-362.

Nasta, T. (2007) Translating national standards into practice for the initial training of further education (FE) teachers, *Research in Post-compulsory education 12*, no 1: 1-17.

O'Neill, O. (2002) Reith Lecture 2002 available at www.bbc.coc.uk/radio4/reith2002 (accessed 1/04/09).

Silverman, D. (2004) *Doing Qualitative Research: A Practical Handbook*, (4th edn). London: Sage Publications.

UCLan, (2008) *Programme Handbook Certificate in Education/PGCE.*

'Am I still a teacher?'

Alison Barton

This chapter aims to answer the question 'Am I still a teacher?' To do this it will explore a specific aspect of teaching (keeping up to date with and disseminating knowledge) while making links with Bloom's Taxonomy of Learning (Bloom, 1956) in the Cognitive Domain.

Setting the Context

I am currently employed by a university (HEI) as a Principal Lecturer in Teacher Education. Analysing my own role led to some interesting insights into the job that I do on behalf of the HEI and also the partner colleges within my network. It seems that I have two main areas of focus, both equally important.

Looking out and across at national issues and agenda, a large part of my role is to sit on committees and work with external organisations to keep up to date with government policy and new initiatives and practice. For this reason I am a member of the Universities Council for the Education of Teachers UCET (Post 16 committee) where I meet other leaders of teacher education partnerships three times each year and take part in their annual conference. This committee is central to the success of my job as the chair of the committee sits on Government working parties and has direct contact with MP's and Cabinet Ministers. By being an active part of this committee I can be sure that the information I receive and have to act on, is accurate and current. In today's changing political climate it helps me to make sensible decisions concerning where the changes in our practice have to take place.

Another really useful aspect of this committee is that it is a place for real discussion about teacher education to occur. With as many as 35 members coming to every meeting and so many different educational philosophies represented we are often engaged in fierce and challenging debate about how to collectively take reform forward. We do not always agree but the debate gives insight and real opportunities to develop personal understanding and shape practice. The committee also supports each other in undertaking validation of new awards and acting as external examiners (critical friends) for other universities. This is a real opportunity for professional development to take place and everyone benefits from seeing other teacher education programmes and sharing ideas.

As well as being a member of the UCET committee I also work with the Office for Educational Standards (Ofsted) at national events to ensure that as a partnership we are accurately interpreting the inspection requirements for trainee teachers. The process is usually one of open discussion and consultation followed by the implementation of policy. Within my role it is important therefore that I take part in consultation events and also make the views of our partnership heard nationally prior to policy and practice being established. This also ensures that when many voices are heard then policy does get changed. This happened recently with the new inspection practice when we encouraged Ofsted to use separate criteria for the four inspection grades for trainee teachers other than those used for qualified and experienced teachers within the sector.

One final area of external and national focus that I need to keep in touch with is Lifelong Learning UK (LLUK) and its endorsing arm Standards Verification UK (SVUK). These bodies have written the national standards and assessment criteria against which all of the qualifications identified within the new regulatory framework are endorsed ensuring that all of the awards offered within the partnership are nationally recognised and valid. I take responsibility for leading the endorsement process and completing all relevant documentation and also for ensuring that colleges work within the parameters of the endorsed awards.

As I write the above it could seem that my job is very focused at a national level away from the practicalities of the delivery of teacher education across the partnership. It may seem boring to be involved in this policy driven practice but actually it is anything but. Positioned between HE and the national committees and organisations I work with, gives me a very wide and long term view of the changes that are coming into teacher education and the opportunity to influence them. Change is rapid and sometimes unnecessary but it always needs managing effectively if we are to remain successful. In this position I can see more of the future of teacher education than the practitioners in the classroom. Looking out to the national picture allows me to 'read the runes' quickly and fine tune our practice to ensure continued success. This is often frustrating, but it is always dynamic and in many ways the fine tuning process is a creative one that allows for the organic development of systems, procedures and practice. It feels a little like navigating through slightly choppy waters having read the instruments well, rather than facing straight into the storm. It is exciting and it is a responsibility.

Successful change though needs to be introduced through a process of ownership. Leaders who stand at the front and dictate change may get compliance but not necessarily commitment from the very people who need to take that change successfully forward. My role within the university then is to operate successfully at the HEI/national interface and also at the higher education (HE) and further education (FE) interface.

Managing a partnership that crosses the two distinct boundaries of HE/FE is a challenging and exciting activity. Historically the cultures of both are distinctly different. Prior to being employed with an HEI I taught on a range of vocational and academic programmes within FE for 20 years. Like many entrants to FE teaching I had also spent many years practising my subject in the 'real world'. The culture of FE has and still is a culture of performance and product, due to contracted working hours and the often vocational nature of training. The focus is firmly on teaching and learning with little time left for professional development

except around curriculum updating. Teachers working within the sector have strong professional identities related to their curriculum area expertise and often struggle to develop a professional identity as an educator. This limited perception of the professional identity also limits both personal and sector aspirations.

The culture of HE however has been very firmly fixed in developing curriculum expertise and new knowledge through the undertaking of scholarly and research activity, the outcomes of which drive the curriculum offered and the professional identity of the lecturers who aspire to create knowledge and have ownership of it. Being employed in one context but managing the other set me the challenge of how to ensure that decisions are taken collectively and collaboratively by everyone who is involved in the teacher educator teams.

First steps in this process focus on removing the boundaries that surround us. Boundaries can be seen as lines of demarcation that clearly identify the differences that exist on either side of the line. Crossing boundaries with different cultures is often difficult and challenging as there needs to be a sensitive acceptance and valuing of each culture: treading carefully and respectfully is required. In our practice we have removed the concept of the boundary and replaced it with an interface that allows us to travel freely in both directions as required. Colleagues from FE therefore work on committees and development groups within HE to develop our programmes and curriculum. They work alongside HE staff at all evaluation and external examiner events in each others colleges and operate in geographical cluster groups offering support and guidance to each other. We are collaborative but not competitive.

However interfaces alone are not enough. An interface allows for movement to take place but it is often movement in and out of differing cultures, after which individuals return to one or another. What the flexible nature of the interface has really achieved is the creation of a working space where individuals and groups can teach and study together effectively. Creating a working space that is neither HE nor FE but a shared place to develop our curriculum and ourselves as practitioners has been one of the unexpected realisations and outcomes of the collaborative nature of our partnership.

So with an eye looking to external policy and regulation my feet are firmly embedded within an HE/FE interface that is a cauldron of discussion, debate and eventual decision making shaped by the information I bring from the larger national agenda. This interface is very much my classroom and my learners are my colleagues from the teacher education teams within each college in the partnership. I use the word 'teacher' and 'learner' with real hesitation here. I am much more a facilitator and we are all learners who often teach each other and learn from the process. In this interface the lines between teaching and learning have become blurred, but teaching is going on and learning and new understanding and knowledge comes about as a result. The interface is our classroom and I am going to present an argument that despite being a manager it is the pedagogic nature of this interface that reveals my position as a teacher.

A process of teaching and learning

At this point I want to stop and consider one example of what the process of teaching and learning might be described as. This will be done against the six levels of the cognitive domain as identified by Bloom in 1956. The six levels are stated as follows:

Knowledge

Comprehension

Application

Analysis

Synthesis

Evaluation

These six statements are often found in teacher training text books (Petty, 2004; Curzon, 2003; Fawbert, 2003; Walkin, 1994) along with explanations of the other domains (Psychomotor and Affective). However the taxonomies did not just emerge from Bloom's work, but from the collective exploration from 1949 - 1956 from 33 other researchers who defined and classified educational goals (Bloom, 1956).

Many of us are familiar with the six words listed above, but very few of us have read Bloom's original text in which each statement is expanded to give a very clear picture of what can be attributed to each stage of the domain. On looking at the original work it became very clear that the activities I undertake as a manager fit very nicely into the expanded discussion presented by Bloom. Bloom introduces the Cognitive Domain as:

> *...including those objectives which deal with the recall or recognition of knowledge and the development of intellectual abilities and skills.*

(Bloom, 1956: 7)

In the next section of this chapter I am going to review my current role within HE and the management of the partnership against the six areas of the cognitive domain to argue that there is a strong pedagogic nature to this work despite it being set within a management and leadership context.

Knowledge

Higher Education places a great deal of importance on 'Knowledge'. In my current role I am required to keep up to date concerning my particular field of work (teacher education for the post compulsory sector) and this section of the taxonomy is very helpful in establishing the role of knowledge in my practice. Bloom argues there are lots of different ways in which something can be 'known' and can depend on 'external authority' and individual or groups of experts. This relates well to the large part of my job which involves

keeping up to date with new government policy and legislation, the requirements of external agencies we are accountable to (Ofsted and SVUK) and new theories and approaches to teaching and learning that may impact on the design of our curriculum. As I acquire new knowledge through reading, attending meetings and my own research Bloom suggests that '*with an increase in knowledge or information there is a development of ones acquaintance with reality*' (Bloom, 1956: 32). Managing a partnership within an ever changing climate of teacher education requires us to collectively solve the problems that emerge. To do this we must all have knowledge of the realities 'out there' and it is my job to seek and find that knowledge to share with colleagues when working at our interface and identify appropriate responses.

Further examination of this domain expands on this more fully and shows the intricacies that are involved here. Bloom recognises certain aspects within this stage that have a significant place in my own practice. He explains that I need to recall '*specific and isolable bits of information*' and have a knowledge of '*specific facts and terminology*', '*conventions and rules for presentation*', '*suitable methodologies*' and with my eye on the big picture, knowledge of '*trends*' that may be emerging. All of this seems very familiar to me when reading government policy and legislation and searching for the important facts and recommendations that will impact on our provision. Knowing conventions and rules for presentation has been essential in completing endorsement documents for SVUK and more recently writing a Self Evaluation Document (SED) on behalf of our partnership for the new Ofsted inspection regime the 'Framework for the inspection of initial teacher education' (Ofsted, 2008). Without the acquisition of this knowledge I could not set up the systems and procedures or the practice that is required of us to comply with the external accountability placed on us.

Comprehension

Exploring this aspect of the domain '*an understanding of the literal message contained within a communication*' (Bloom, 1956: 89) is even more enlightening. Bloom explains three different types of comprehension that can be identified within the taxonomy. The first, '*translation*' recognises the capacity to communicate to others by using a separate language or another form of communication, the knowledge that has been received. He suggests this may result in knowledge being moved from an abstract to a concrete form. I can recognise myself doing this as words become tables or models or flow diagrams to make them more accessible to everyone in the partnership. The second '*interpretation*' requires me to explain to others the relevant importance of ideas and also the interrelated nature of what is said in one document but has an impact on the working practice of another. I know that I am very careful in undertaking this activity to ensure that my interpretation is accurate by checking out with external agencies the significance of facts and ideas presented. Finally Bloom identifies that '*extrapolation*' is also a demonstration of

comprehension. I have to really be able to extrapolate forward and make predications based on the knowledge I hold concerning the implications and consequences for the partnership and its trainee teachers of not taking appropriate action. Comprehension then really requires me to think about the knowledge I have gleaned, be able to share this in an accessible format with my colleagues, see the impact of separate pieces of policy and legislation in operation together and therefore predict the changes we need to introduce to offer successful programmes.

Application

Bloom identifies the significance of application relating to real life:

> *...the fact that most of what we learn is intended for application to problem situations in real life is indicative of the importance of application.*

(Bloom, 1956: 122)

Some key words stand out for me in the quote above, *'application' 'problem situations'* and *'real life'*. All of the knowledge and learning I complete and all of the thought process and internalisation of that knowledge is only useful if it can be used to transform and have an impact on the problems we face as a partnership in the real world of teaching and learning in the lifelong learning sector. Armed with information I can understand the systems and procedures that I know need to be introduced into practice, it is my responsibility to 'make it happen'. This aspect of the taxonomy is one that for me carries significant creativity with it. Application is often a design process and all of the curriculum is designed and then redesigned to meet the needs of external agencies, to reflect current educational practice and to reflect the value base of the teacher education teams who deliver awards. All associated documentation is developed to be effective in use and reflexive in purpose to account for meeting local needs in delivering awards. My role is to design and develop the working documents that record our practice and shape the materials that everyone uses keeping an eye to external accountability and also responding to feedback from the teachers and·learners who are part of the process.

Up to this point I have been operating in a managerial and external environment away from the partnership interface. Knowledge has been acquired, appropriate interpretations made and suitable curriculum, documentation, systems and procedures created that are disseminated for others to put into practice. Our external accountability can be met. However, the final stages of the taxonomy illustrate very well the processes engaged with in a partnership where collegiality is significant and where our understanding of who we are accountable to is not just external agencies. As a community of practitioners working together we have an internal accountability to each other and also to our trainees and their learners. If the first three stages of the taxonomy are personal to me then the final three stages are applied collectively to everyone in the partnership and used as strategies to

develop our practice when we meet. We move out of the managerial environment into a broader collective learning environment where learning is collaborative and facilitated.

Analysis

If comprehension illustrates our grasp of meaning and application demonstrates our use of key principles in creative ways and this is carried out by a single individual who is managing, then analysis:

> *emphasises the breakdown of the material into its constituent parts and the detection of the relationships of the parts and the way they are organised.*
>
> (Bloom, 1956: 144)

I have included the quote from Bloom as it is a lovely demonstration of what we carry out collectively within the partnership. At some stage what has been designed must be challenged, considered and deconstructed to make sure that it will be workable in practice. As a group we analyse new curricula, systems, procedures, policy and practice from three different perspectives all identified by Bloom within this area of the domain. We initially look at the different *elements* of what is being offered, asking the questions: What is missing? What could be removed? What could be clearer or needs developing? Then we look at the *relationships* between *elements*. Are they connected appropriately and how are they organised together? What are the arrangements and structures provided and are they logical, sequential and developmental? Do they allow for flexibility and creativity?

This analysis is always mindful of the situation into which any materials will be used and is brought about through myself and colleagues facilitating group work, discussion and problem solving activities where the shared analysis of many colleagues who are involved in teacher education gives a very realistic picture of the real situations involved. Often we try to use these activities to identify problems before they occur in practice, but in reality we also provide opportunity to repeat analysis after we have tried things out so that the analysis becomes part of a 'fine tuning' process.

Synthesis

Bloom explains synthesis as *'...putting together of elements and parts to form a whole'* (Bloom, 1956: 162). What is valuable to us in the partnership is that this reconstruction takes place by many different people and so the final 'whole' is potentially different to what was originally presented at the application stage and is the result of input from all participants. It is a shared reconstruction that reflects collective thinking. This process has been used consistently and successfully within our partnership to meet the challenges of introducing the reform agenda, create new modules and qualifications, design handbooks and paperwork and respond to feedback from external examiners. Bloom recognises that

this part of the taxonomy '*…most clearly provides for creative behaviour*' (Bloom, 1956: 162) and this is evident within the partnership as we put together unique materials from our collective insights. Typically engaging with this process gives an ownership of the final products that can only come from personalised adaptation and is a real benefit to us all as we implement curricula and documents across our provision.

Evaluation

As I write this chapter I realise that a lot of what is undertaken in relation to this taxonomy occurs in separate blocks of time. Evaluation can follow immediately from synthesis as we check out if our collective understanding will actually work when applied into practice. More often though we implement action and then reflect on the outcomes, evaluating success or problems to draw new insight and conclusions often on an individual basis that are then brought back to be discussed within the partnership. Evaluation is often formal through module evaluations and accreditation panel meetings with learners and teachers, feedback from external examiners and endorsement reviewers and from our own critical reflection on our practice. Bloom recognises that in evaluation we are checking out the 'value' of something, we ask questions, like how accurate? How effective? How economical? And how satisfying has this been. We look for where improvements can and should be made and in the cyclical nature of all learning we bring this new knowledge back into the partnership to discuss with our colleagues to constantly fine tune, sharpen and nurture the provision we offer.

Reflection

When I started this chapter I asked the question 'Am I still a Teacher?' Employed as a Manager, positioned as a leader and with very little formal teaching activity on my timetable many would conclude that the answer to the question is No.

When I was a Teacher Educator I really loved the sessions I did teaching Bloom's Taxonomy because for me it represents a key that opens the door to a depth of thinking about the teaching and learning process that many find easy to access. At a critical moment in our sessions we used to ask what is it that teachers do? And often arrived at the conclusions that they:

Acquire *knowledge* about their subject.

Internalise and *comprehend* their learning.

Create teaching resources and teaching strategies, *application*.

Ask questions and challenge perceptions *analysis*,.

Build old knowledge into new and reconstruct their learning *synthesis*.

Check learning for accuracy and clarity *evaluating*.

At an even more critical moment we asked the same question concerning learners, what is going on for learners in a learning situation? We agreed that learners receive new *(knowledge)* from a wide range of resources including the teacher, internalise and add it to their understanding *(comprehension)* and were facilitated to *(apply)* learning to a range of situations. They were required to deconstruct what had been learnt, challenging it *(analysis)* before having their own light bulb moment when they could 'see it now' *(synthesis)* prior to checking out if the conclusions they had drawn, the picture they could see was accurate *(evaluation)*.

Many light bulb moments in our session resulted in a realisation that teaching was in fact learning, and learning was in fact teaching, having a profound impact on how we design learning situations for future groups. Undertaking the analysis of Bloom to write this chapter has made it clear to me that I 'feel' like a teacher because I am using the process described above when I work with my colleagues from across our partnership. When I read back through the sections it feels like such a rosy and perfect picture to have painted but like all real life teaching situations it is fraught with difficulty and uncertainty.

The knowledge I seek is often difficult to read and access, I am making meaning out of material that is complicated to understand and concerns driving forward agenda I personally may not want to undertake. It is a singular and often lonely process. Making sense of it all requires a commitment to the partnership and a passion for education that allows me to see the potential good in what needs to be undertaken. Designing and creating documents and practice to respond to policy on behalf of others can be exciting as I 'drill down' into what is really important, but is equally scary as I check to make sure I have 'got it right'. Stopping here would be good enough for many, it would be easy just to send out the materials and say 'get on with it' but a learning community requires us all to embrace new knowledge and practice and collectively understand the reasons for change and movement and the need to move out of comfort zones into new places. I said earlier that implementation without a process of shared analysis just leads to compliance and in the end compliance is not quality, compliance is conformity and this is always mediocre.

A desire for quality and excellence in education requires commitment and somehow through a teaching process I have to enable occasionally reluctant colleagues to embrace new knowledge and practice and use it with confidence. This can only be achieved by allowing analysis of what is presented to take place. Accompanied by challenge and reconstruction this often means that what has been developed is discarded, changed, altered, improved and then after implementation and evaluation, is changed again. This can be frustrating and difficult, sometimes heated but always alive and dynamic. In this environment I need to rethink, relearn, respond in a different way, I am thinking and learning, learning and thinking just like everyone else involved in the process.

So am I still a teacher? Bloom's Taxonomy has helped me to confidently answer Yes to this question as I use the tools of a teacher to support and develop teacher education. Bloom also reminds me though that I am also a learner, and despite the challenges that both of these roles bring I would not have it any other way.

References

Bloom, S. (1956) *Taxonomy of Educational Objectives Book 1*, Cognitive Domain. New York: David McKay Company.

Curzon, L. B. (2004) *Teaching in Further Education an Outline of Principles and Practice*, (6th edn). London: Continuum.

DfES (2004) *Equipping our Teachers for the Future*. London: HMSO.

DfES (2006) *Further Education: Raising Skills, Improving Life Chances.* London: HMSO.

Fawbert, F. (Ed.) (2003) *Teaching in Post Compulsory Education Learning, Skills and Standards.* London: Continuum.

Institute for Learning (IfL) http://www.ifl.ac.uk

Lifelong Learning UK (LLUK) *New overarching professional standards for teacher, tutors and trainers in the lifelong learning sector*: available online: http://www.lifelonglearninguk.org

Ofsted (2005) *Framework for the inspection of initial teacher training for the award of qualified teacher status* 2005–11 (HMI 2446) available on line: www.ofsted.gov.uk/publications

Ofsted (2008) *Framework for the inspection of initial teacher education 2008* available on line: www.ofsted.gov.uk/publications

Ofsted (2008) *Grade criteria for the inspection of initial teacher education 2008–11*

available on line: www.ofsted.gov.uk/publications

OPSI (2007) *Further Education Teachers' Qualifications (England) Regulations 2007* (the 2007 Regulations) available online: http://www.opsi.gov.uk

OPSI (2007) *The Further Education Teachers' Continuing Professional Development and Registration (England) Regulations 2007,* (2007 No. 2116). available online: http://www.opsi.gov.uk

Petty, G. (2004) *Teaching Today,* (3rd edn). Cheltenham: Nelson Thornes.

Walkin, L. (1994) *Teaching and Learning in Further and Adult Education*. Cheltenham: Stanley Thornes.